## ALL TWC

## *Artificial Intelligence Python:*

*A short Introduction to Artificial Intelligence with Python*

## *Reinforcement Learning with Python:*

*A short Overview of Reinforcement Learning with Python*

*By Anthony S. Williams*

# Artificial Intelligence Python

A short Introduction to Artificial Intelligence with Python

*By Anthony S. Williams*

© Copyright 2017 by Anthony S. Williams - All rights reserved.

Respective authors own all copyrights not held by the publisher.

The following publication is reproduced below with the goal of providing information that is as accurate and reliable as possible. Regardless, purchasing this publication can be seen as consent to the fact that both the publisher and the author of this book are in no way experts on the topics discussed within and that any recommendations or suggestions that are made herein are for informational purposes only. Professionals should be consulted as needed prior to undertaking any of the action endorsed herein.

This declaration is deemed fair and valid by both the American Bar Association and the Committee of Publishers Association and is legally binding throughout the United States.

Furthermore, the transmission, duplication or reproduction of any of the following work including specific information will be considered an illegal act irrespective of if it is done electronically or in print. This extends to creating a secondary or tertiary copy of the work or a recorded copy and is only allowed with express written consent from the Publisher. All additional right reserved.

The information in the following pages is broadly considered to be a truthful and accurate account of facts and as such any inattention, use or misuse of the information in question by the reader will render any resulting actions solely under their purview. There are no scenarios in which the publisher or the original author of this work can be in any fashion deemed liable for any hardship or damages that may befall them after undertaking information described herein.

Additionally, the information in the following pages is intended only for informational purposes and should thus be thought of as universal. As befitting its nature, it is presented without assurance regarding its prolonged validity or interim quality. Trademarks that are mentioned are done without written consent and can in no way be considered an endorsement from the trademark holder.

The trademarks that are used are without any consent, and the publication of the trademark is without permission or backing by the trademark owner. All trademarks and brands within this book are for clarifying purposes only and are the owned by the owners themselves, not affiliated with this document.

# Table of Contents

Introduction ................................................................ 1

**Chapter 1 Approaches and Goals of Artificial Intelligence** ................................................................ 6

    Origins of Artificial Intelligence .......................................... 7

    The Research Goals of Artificial Intelligence ................ 15

    Approaches to Defining AI Systems ............................... 23

**Chapter 2 Fundamental AI Techniques** .................... 28

    Heuristics ............................................................................ 28

    Support Vector Machines ................................................. 35

    Artificial Neural Networks ............................................... 39

    Markov Decision Process ................................................. 41

    Natural Language Processing .......................................... 45

**Chapter 3 Artificial Intelligence Methodology** .......... 50

    Reinforcement Learning ................................................... 50

    Regression and Classification .......................................... 57

    Clustering Algorithms ...................................................... 59

**Chapter 4 Build a Recommender Systems** ................ 63

    Automatic Speech Recognition ....................................... 66

**Chapter 5 Genetic and Logic Programming** ............. 69

**Conclusion** ................................................................ 76

# Introduction

Artificial intelligence or simply AI is known as the field of machine learning. The term is referred to the intelligence notably exhibited by various machines rather than humans. The intelligence exhibited by humans is referred to as natural intelligence or NI. When it comes to the computer science, the certain field of artificial intelligence mainly defines itself as the overall study of different intelligent agents or devices specifically able to perceive their environment as well as to take different actions, which maximize the chance of success when it comes to the certain goal.

The term artificial intelligence colloquially is commonly applied in the cases when a machine or device mimics various cognitive functions which humans commonly associate with some other human minds like problem-solving and learning. The overall scope of artificial intelligence is widely disputed since machines, especially in recent times, become increasingly capable. This means that the tasks notably considered as those that require intelligence are commonly removed from the AI definition. This is known as the artificial intelligence effect widely leading to the severe grip, so we consider the AI field as everything that has not been done yet. For example, the field optical character recognition is commonly excluded from AI since it has become a certain routine technology.

When it comes to the certain capabilities of the artificial intelligence, they include competing at a high level when it comes to the strategic game systems like Go and chess, successfully understanding human speech, autonomous cars, military simulations, intelligent routing when it comes to the content delivery networks and interpreting various complex data.

Artificial intelligence, in fact, was founded as an academic discipline back in 1956. In the following years, AI has been the subject of major waves of optimism and various experiments and researches. However, in the very beginning, artificial intelligence was followed by great disappointment as well as the loss of funding specifically known as an AI winter that has been followed by some modern approaches which eventually led to renewed function.

For most of AI history, artificial intelligence field has been divided into certain subfields which often greatly fail in order to communicate with each other which is the key concept of any field. However, in the early 21st century several statistical approaches to machine learning were able to become successful enough in order to eclipse several other tools, problems, approaches and schools of thought which served as a fertile ground for further development and integration of various artificial intelligence approaches.

The traditional problems, as well as goals of artificial intelligence research, include natural language processing, reasoning, planning, learning, knowledge and the ability and perception when it comes to the moving and manipulating objects. General intelligence is the field with the long-term goals and its approaches include traditional symbolic artificial intelligence, statistical methods, and computational intelligence. When it comes to the tools commonly used in the fields of AI, they include different versions of mathematical and search optimization, methods based on statistics, neural networks, economics as well as probability.

The artificial intelligence field notably draws upon computer science, philosophy, neuroscience, psychology, linguistics, artificial psychology as well as many others. The field of artificial intelligence was founded on the various claims that human intelligence is a kind that can be described very precisely, so a machine or device is able to simulate human intelligence. This, in fact, raises various philosophical arguments when it comes to the nature of the human mind as well as various arguments about the ethics of creating some artificial beings notably with human-like intelligence.

There are many issues regarding the creation of these human-like devices and machines, which raise many issues that have been explored by philosophy, myth as well as fiction since antiquity. There are some people that consider AI approaches and methods as a certain danger to humanity in a case if AI progresses unabatedly.

In the 21st century, various artificial intelligence techniques and methods have experienced certain resurgence mainly following concurrent advances in terms of computer power, big data, and theoretical understanding. Many AI methods and techniques recently have become a very significant as well as among the essential parts of the overall technology industry. AI techniques are those notably helping when it comes to the solving various challenging problems especially when it comes to the computer science.

| **Artificial Intelligence** ||
| --- | --- |
| Research Fields | Research Techniques |
| Intelligent Machine | Artificial Neural Networks |
| Knowledge Representation | Evolutionary Computing |
| Machine Learning | Expert Systems |
| Computer Vision | Fuzzy Logic |
| Planning and Guidance | Genetic Algorithm |
| Robotics | Probabilistic Computing |

When it comes to the main goals of AI, the first one I have to mention is to create technology, which allows machines and computers to function in a certain intelligent manner. However, the general problem of creating or simulating intelligence commonly has been broken down into some sub-problems notably consisting of capabilities as well as certain traits specifically expected by the researchers when it comes to the displaying an intelligent system.

The greatest emphasize in on the learning and planning which are relevant as well as easily applicable to various situations. In the following sections of the book, goals of the AI are discussed as well as various AI approaches.

# Chapter 1 Approaches and Goals of Artificial Intelligence

Over the course of the last sixty years, the AI research field greatly spurred some immense features notably those which are not conceived as artificial intelligence by the general public. Majority of online endeavors include different forms of artificial intelligence like targeted advertising, pattern recognition, and various virtual agents. However, all that has been greatly done so far. Therefore, we need to acquire new knowledge on the different processes in order to position ourselves in accordance to these advancements.

When it comes to the importance of AI techniques, for instance, the business enterprise has become aware that AI methods and techniques can be and most certainly will be in the future a certain definitive factor when it comes to the overall success. These various properties currently are widely implemented in different data analysis algorithms that have a great capability when it comes to the properly storing, analyzing as well as processing Big Data that is another growing sector of business management. These recent approaches are expected to soon include different product optimization algorithms as well as complex customer engagement methods and techniques.

## Origins of Artificial Intelligence

Foundations of different ideas revolving around the origins of AI can be tracked down to complex automation built by Chinese and Egyptian civilizations as well as to Greek mythology. Implementing various human properties to different objects as well as implementing abstract ideas is a certain way people have been reasoning since the very beginning of human existence as soon as they acquired consciousness.

With the emergence of the complex symbolic reasoning as well as with the development of logic, the creation of devices and machines which could emulate complex human intelligence became possible as well as achievable in practice. When it comes to the symbolic reasoning, it states that various symbols including numbers, calculations, statistics, and graphs can be easily used as certain synonymous substitutes for some longer expressions to solve different complex problems. This idea was introduced back in the 16th century by the Grandfather of artificial intelligence, Thomas Hobbes.

Further, when it comes to the origins of artificial intelligence methods since engineering advanced increasingly over the centuries, the fields of AI and engineering began to greatly correlate. The first computer was designed back in the 19th century, but it was not built until 1991. People were aware of the ongoing process when it comes to the technological advancements in the early 20th century. They also understood the increasing necessity of understanding the processes of device computing and various models which led to creating of different theoretical discourses.

When it comes to the origins of artificial intelligence, I have to mention Alan Turing who published a fundamental work on this subject back in 1950 named the Computing Machinery and Intelligence paper. In his paper, Alan proposed certain Turing machine model. In his paper, his further discussed various theoretical possibilities of different things notably what can be easily computed. He created the Turing test in order to deduct whether various computing possibilities can extend to the different spheres in terms of human intelligence.

The Turing test, proposed by Alan has an objective to test as well as to identify whether a device or machine can convince an interrogator that it was a human being. The test initially seemed to be very simple with no complex assignments like creating original art.

Further, the computer was able to perform a small talk in order to pass the test. The computer also was able to understand the given context while interacting with a human. It really sounds very simple from our perspective, but the actual realization of such results proved to be more complex and difficult than anticipated and this complexity remained up to this date. It, in fact, is unachievable.

Primary problems related to different hardware technology when it comes to the 20th century are complex storage room issues that camouflaged complex future issues in terms of software realization. Researchers are still trying to design software which would pass Alan's Turing test. The Leobner prize is still waiting for the software which would be able to pass the test and we hope to see one in the near future presented in the annual Turing Competition.

Artificial intelligence is the field of study based on different mathematical, philosophical, logical, cybernetic and information technology advancements. This field of study was born in 1956 with experts Marvin Minsky and John McCarthy which introduced this new study at a conference which took place at Dartmouth College. They became very prominent name when it comes to the wide-spanning effort in order to create intelligent devices and machines for the following fifty years.

In order to create intelligence, an expert first has to know and understand what intelligence is. On the other hand, some abstract definitions of intelligence state that intelligence is a property of human beings and some animals that are commonly manifested in learning through experience, reasoning, logic, an appliance of knowledge, creativity and other. This definition also states that it cannot be simply translated into some symbols and that it cannot produce sentient machinery.

Scientists were able to implement different approaches and techniques in order to build up complex artificial intelligence. One of the used approaches is the evolution of the complex chess-playing software. The fact is that it was much easier to achieve great efficiency through some brute force techniques notably meaning that the machine or computer is able to compute solution algorithms based on the principle of minimal cost when there is the maximum damage possible for a particular amount of all future moves. The chess-playing software, in fact, did not focus that greatly on building different sentiment, but it focused on some advanced search techniques as well as on to sustainable hardware for huge databases.

However, expert systems were developed in order to provide a greater expert assistance in various industries. By creating these proficient knowledge databases as well as by incorporating different machine learning software that enables devices and machines to make a various prediction as well as to provide consultation regarding obtained data, a scientist was able to broaden the properties when it comes to their intelligent devices and machines. Interaction software developed is based on natural language development, and all further achievements have been used in navigation systems, business management as well as in medicine to these days.

It should be noted that after the initial exhilaration within the artificial intelligence research, it soon was more than apparent that various solid results, in fact, are going to take more than previously expected and announced. Lighthill and ALPAC report clearly showed great unsatisfactory when it comes to the AI projects at the very beginning mainly due to issues with slow advancements and various natural language problems. At the time the flux of huge investments was terminated in 1974. There were no any investments to AI projects until the early 1980s when the British government decided to instigate different artificial intelligence projects in order to respond to various Japanese endeavors regarding their logic programming.

However, due to the collapses regarding the general-purpose computer market, there was a decrease in investing and funding the second Winter of AI event in 1987. In this winter periods, artificial intelligence research continued under some different names which eventually became sub-categories of the AI field including machine learning, data mining, speech recognition, industrial robotics, evolutionary programming, search engines and many other.

The main question is where is artificial intelligence these days? In order to answer this question, you just have to look around you and you will see that AI techniques and the overall artificial intelligence research enabled a great progress that is regarded common these days. The artificial intelligence research enabled specified as well as personalized search engine results, vehicle navigation systems, intelligent personal assistant software like Google Translate and Siri, diverse robotics advancements and enhancements and many other.

When it comes to the some of the most notable achievements of artificial approach and techniques, I have to mention IBM's Deep Blue which became the first computer that was able to a win a chess game against Garry Kasparov who is a chess champion. Another great achievement is IBM's complex question answerings system named Watson notably able of winning the Jeopardy quiz against some very proficient opponents back in 2011.

It is more than apparent that some hard issues of AI have not seen immense progress when it comes to the last fifty years. At the moment, many experts and scientist involved in AI projects predict at least fifty more years of error and trial in order to successfully emulate human intelligence. It is too broad as well as to complex of a subject in order to resolve in a short period of time. On the other hand, the advances which were made during the last fifty years have greatly influenced as well as shaped the world we live in. There are also many chances yet to come since the fields of AI are being explored increasingly especially when it comes to the recent years.

**Artificial Intelligence Timeline:**

- Programmable mechanical calculating machine-1842
- Turing test by Alan Turing-1950
- Artificial intelligence and the first conference by Malvin Nimsky and John McCarthy-1956
- General problem solver demonstrated on by Newell-1957
- Industrial robot working on GE-1961
- ELIZA and the first expert system introduced by Joseph Waizenbau-1965
- MacHack chess-playing programm at MIT-1968
- Knowledge-based medical diagnosis program by Jack Myers-1979
- Commercial expert system-1980s
- Behaviour-based robotics Polly by Ian Horswill-1993
- Recommendation technology by TiVo Suggestions-2005
- Mobile recommendation apps Cortana, Siri and Now by Microsoft, Apple and Google-2011
- Machine learning and deep learning-present day

# The Research Goals of Artificial Intelligence

When it comes to the overall research goal of AI, it is to create an intelligent device or machine notably capable of planning, reasoning and solving various problems. The created machine should be able to learn from experience as well as to learn quickly and comprehend various complex ideas. Learning from experience and capability of planning, reasoning, thinking abstractly and learning quickly is an agreed definition of human intelligence. In practice, artificially emulated intelligence is mainly to reflect a certain broad as well as a deep ability in order to comprehend its environment and surrounding and to figure out what to do next when there are infinite possible situations.

The artificial intelligence needs to be widely socially intelligent in order to position itself in different environments. This means that AI has to be able to widely perceive as well as to properly react to some broad spectra of different abstract features as well as properties of the universe like emotion. The artificial intelligence also needs to have a capability of implementing creativity when it comes to its functioning in order to manage various problems in an optimal manner and anticipated manner. All of these needed properties are further attributed to the overall as well as to the final goal of every AI research and study.

In order to achieve any goal when it comes to the AI research, experts and scientist have to mainly focus on a huge portfolio of different and complex concepts which are notably different blocks existing individually as well as in correlation. The builders when it comes to the future intelligent machine, need to successfully implement their work into some empirical steeds of already existing intelligent systems specifically systems in term of human beings as well as we the results of different theoretical exploration and different analysis of various possible systems of intelligence including their representations and mechanism.

The factors from the previous paragraph, in fact, are the most essential when it comes to the finding a resolution of issues notably related to some already existing intelligent system. These factors are the most relevant and of great importance when it comes to the designing some entirely new intelligent as well as some semi-intelligent devices and machines. This means that the complexity of any task has to be acquired since by restricting different endeavors to just one field like engineering, the overall efforts commonly will not provide much-anticipated results. The most obvious example is that is would have been impossible to construct plane without examination of birds, and when it comes to the AI, the situation is the same, and scientists need to explore different fields of AI in order to get the anticipated results.

**Goals of Artificial Intelligence:**

- Deduction, reasoning and problem solving
- Knowledge representation
- Planning
- Learning
- Natural language processing
- Motion and manipulation
- Perception
- Creativity
- Social intelligence
- General intelligence

The main goals of AI have presented above. It is the right time to get to know these goals a little better in order to understand AI approach better before we step into the real world of problem-solving using AI techniques. In the beginning of artificial intelligence research, the overall reasoning process induced by step by step imitation of different human processing in terms of logical deduction and solving puzzles.

However, this certain approach greatly depended on various computation resources as well as on computer memory which ate at the time greatly confined. These issues, in fact, pointed out the great necessity existing when it comes to the imitation as well as immediate judgment process rather than a necessity of deliberate reasoning. Immediate judgment may be seen as subconscious knowledge and as well as the intuitive knowledge that governs the direction of every deliberate action.

Artificial intelligence makes different attempts at reaching its goals especially when it comes to the immediate judgment using the combination of sensorimotor skills, embodied agents, neural networks, and different statistical approaches. For instance, embodied agents are used commonly since they are greatly autonomous entities that have the ability to interact with their surroundings and environment and they are commonly presented as three-dimensional certain robot bodies.

On the other hand, sensorimotor skills are very much needed a combination of skills used when it comes to the perceiving surroundings and environment through various sensors. Sensorimotor skills also include the ability to react with different motor skills. For instance, there is a robot notably able of perceiving an approaching person. The robot is also capable of offering a hand while greeting with the person. Neural networks represent a simulation of different structures as well as processes within the neural systems, notably human brain. Neural networks are able of computing different values obtained from inputs, while machine learning techniques are able of pattern recognition. Experts also use different statistical approaches in order to obtain specific problem resolution using mathematical approach.

Artificial intelligence has to incorporate immense amounts of knowledge regarding different objects and its properties as well as a relation between different objects. Only by doing so, AI is able to emulate a human being. Moreover, artificial intelligence has to implement different states, effects, situation and abstract ideas. The artificial intelligence research field uses a certain ontological approach in order to move towards knowledge representation which is knowledge specifically postulated in different sets of concepts whose relationship is commonly defined within a domain.

There are many issues existing when it comes to the knowledge representation like the impossibility of false or true statement since everything has exceptions. Another issue regarding this subject is the width of overall human knowledge notably making creating more comprehensive ontology almost not possible. Other issues are that sub-symbolic, as well as the subconscious forms of knowledge, needs to be integrated within AI project. Fortunately, these issues may be overcome using AI techniques like statistical AI notably using a mathematical resolution of particular problems. On the other hand, situated AI research uses various systems as autonomous entities through the certain interaction with surroundings in order to develop and obtain Elementary behaviors. Computational intelligence research is creating a computer that can understand concepts, so the computer is able to provide ontology by itself via different ways like the Internet.

It should be noted that AI has to be able to construct various complex as well as optimized solutions when it comes to the multidimensional perform realization and multidimensional space of different sequences or strategies of the overall action. It can be said in another word as well. The intelligent agents have to be able to visualize different potential failures by using predictive analysis. The intelligent agents also have to be able to visualize set goals of the overall action which belong to decision making. From the intelligent agents, it is also expected to perform in a certain manner that will greatly maximize value or efficiency of the overall process.

These goals of artificial intelligence need to be handled both online for different unexpected environments as well as offline for some already known environments. Experts still embark on some great challenges when it comes to the dealing with the issues of various unpredicted scenarios like when the machine is anticipated to react more intelligently.

Artificial intelligence is greatly correlated with the field of machine learning since machine learning is a certain construction as well as a study of different algorithms that allow artificial intelligence systems to make the different decision as well as predictions notably based on obtained data input and certain knowledge specifically acquired through machine learning process. Machine learning techniques may be focused on unsupervised and supervised methods. The unsupervised process is a pattern recognition while supervised or programmer is classification as well as a relation formation within the input data like guiding spam and non-spam emails into certain different categories within the system.

Machine learning is widely used in different spheres when it comes to the information technology. The techniques of machine learning are used in search engines personalization, optical character recognition, computer vision as well as data mining. It is expected that the further enhancements of the approaches will greatly attribute to the computational intelligence of devices and machines.

I have to mention natural language processing and machine perception since these approaches are commonly used in different AI research projects. Natural language processing, as well as generation, are one of the fundamental issues that the AI field of study commonly deals with. On the other hand machine perception widely represents the ability of different input interpretation which resembles processes of different human perception through senses.

The issues which are trying to be addressed and solved are commonly those of transmission to an intelligent core of some entity and comprehensive perception. Machine perception has to deal with different challenges in both computing features and engineering. Machine perception uses touch, vision, and hearing in order to collect different information based on audio and image properties in order to address the to various solutions or algorithms for a certain problem.

## Approaches to Defining AI Systems

From the very beginning of the AI research back in the 1950s, there have been numerous approaches conducted through the implementation of different knowledge in various academic circles and industries. These approaches rapidly evolved as a certain response to some shortcomings which each of them commonly showed especially when it comes to the realization of the ultimate goal notably general intelligence. When the artificial intelligence research lost its findings during the event of AI winters, the great disintegration of different AI approaches was the only possible way in order to acquire some investments for further studies.

From today's point of view, it can be easily concluded that all of the AI approaches are relevant as well as greatly essential when it comes to the vast complexities of AI and all of them served as a great contribution to the overall process regardless of how lacking and slow advancements may be during the overall process. Connectivity approach was used in order to combine knowledge and techniques commonly used in information technology and neurology, so experts were able to achieve a simulation of the most basic intelligence back in the 1950s. Connectivity approach abounded before it has emerged again back in the 1980s. When it comes to the achievements of this approach, I have to mention that the experts were able to gain valuable knowledge on regulatory systems, sensory processing and they were able to better understand the behavior of neural networks.

Another commonly used AI approach is symbolism. This approach states that complexity of human intelligence may be simulated through manipulation of different symbols. The approach had a huge success in high intelligence simulation back in the 1960s. When it comes to the approach achievements, the scientists were able to develop complex expert systems.

Another commonly used approach is a cognitive simulation which is embodied in different psychological tests which were commonly conducted to acquire knowledge of solving skills by a human. The results obtained were formalized in order to develop different programs notably having the ability to simulate certain properties of high human intelligence. The achievements of cognitive simulation approach include the conducting of different foundations for AI research including natural language processing and machine learning.

The logic approach is another commonly used AI approach which has that high human intelligence in its core greatly spurs from different abstract reasoning as well as from problem-solving so it can be treated with different logic's techniques. Achievements of logic approach include automated planning, logic programming, knowledge representation and machine learning.

On the other hand, there is an anti-logic approach which is the complete opposition to the logic approach. This approach states that there is no any general principle notably able of capturing the complexity when it comes to the intelligent behavior. Achievement of the anti-logic approach is that pointed out the great lack of efficiency when it comes to the logic approach especially in a matter of natural language processing and machine vision.

The knowledge-based approach is another approach that was widely implemented in various artificial intelligence studies since the increase of storage capacities and due to the emergence of different expert systems. Knowledge-based approach explored some fundamental elements of general intelligence as well as it was able to implement AI research techniques into expert systems. Another approach commonly used is the abstract approach that emerged from the great necessity of addressing fundamental specters and sub-symbolic specters of human intelligence to provide some optimal solutions for issues and problems of artificial intelligence approach. Abstract approach achievements include robotics, pattern recognition, computer perception and machine learning.

Novel or situated artificial intelligence approach mainly focuses on some basic engineering problems. The approach rejects the exclusivity when it comes to the previous symbolic approach. The ultimate goal is to construct a certain realistic machine which can exist in some real environment. Situated or novel AI approach achievements include computer perception, sensory and motor skills. The last approach I am going to mention is statistical AI approach that uses verifiable and measurable mathematical tools and further combines them with different economics tools to solve a certain AI problem. However, this approach is commonly criticized in terms of disregard towards the ultimate goal of general intelligence. On the other hand, this approach gave scientist the ability to successfully address a certain AI problems.

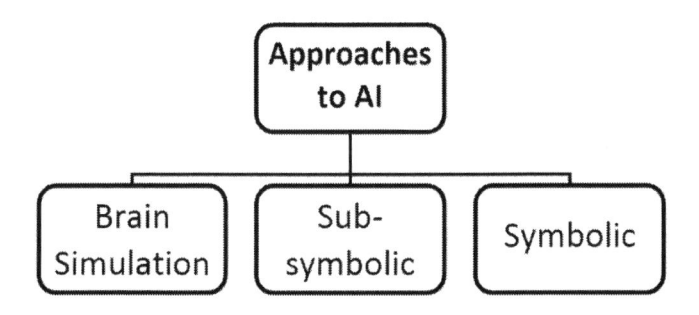

```
                    Approaches
                       to AI
        ┌──────────────┼──────────────┐
    Brain            Sub-           Symbolic
  Simulation       symbolic
```

# Chapter 2 Fundamental AI Techniques

According to a certain area of AI research, there are different techniques commonly used such as natural language processing, intelligent data analysis in medicine, knowledge-base systems, cognitive modeling and other. In this section of the book, we are zooming into fundamental AI techniques in order to get to know the fundamentals of the AI methodology so most certainly you will much closer to the world of the artificial intelligence by the end of this chapter. In this chapter of the book, we will get to know AI techniques including heuristics, support vector machines, artificial neural networks, Markov decision process and natural language processing.

**Heuristics**

Heuristics is a technique or widely used approach when it comes to the learning, problem-solving of just discovery of which employs some practical method, but with no guarantee that the approach will result in a perfect or optimal solution. On the other hand, this AI technique provides sufficient source for some immediate goals. In the cases where finding some optimal solution is almost impossible as well as impractical, this technique is used in order to speed the overall process when it comes to the finding the most satisfactory solution.

Heuristics also may be some mental shortcut. Examples of this AI technique include using guesstimate, common sense, a rule of thumb, intuitive judgment and profiling. Scientists commonly use availability heuristic, representative heuristic, anchoring and adjustment, familiarity, escalation of commitment and naïve diversification. This technique is also found to be used when it comes to the creation and manipulation of cognitive maps. Cognitive maps are some internal representations of the human physical environment, commonly associated with different spatial relationships.

Internal representations of the human environment are widely used as memory when it comes to the guiding different human external environments. In computer science, mathematical optimization and artificial intelligence, this technique is used in order to solve problems in an easier manner and more quickly especially when using some more traditional methods are too slow. Traditional methods may fail when it comes to the finding the exact solution, so heuristic is used in order to minimize the probability of failure notably achieved by completeness, precision for speed, accuracy, and optimality.

The main objective of this technique is to create a solution in some reasonable time frame which is good enough for solving future problems. It should be noted that this solution may not be the best one, but it will be able to approximate the proper solution for a given problem. The technique is very valuable in AI research since it does not require a certain prohibitively long time. The technique is able to produce results by themselves that may be used in different conjunction with various optimization algorithms in order to improve their efficiency. This technique, in fact, underlines the whole world of AI as well as the world of the computer thinking and simulation, since this approach can be used in various situations when there are no any known algorithms.

Further, you will get to know how to create an eight-puzzle solver in Python with plug in heuristics. The model will be able to solve a randomized 8-puzzle.

import random

import math

_goal_state = [[ 1,2,3 ], [ 4,5,6 ], [ 7,8,0 ]]

def index (item, seq

return -1

This is a helper function, which returns -1 for all non-found index value of seq.

def __init__(self)

self._hval = 0

self._depth = 0

self._parent = None

self.adj_matrix = []

self.adj_matrix.append

def __eq__

self.adj_matrix == other.adj_matrix def __str__(self): res = '' for row in range(3): res += ' '.join (map(str, self.adj_matrix[row]))

res += '\r\n' return res def _clone (self):

p = EightPuzzle ()

p.adj_matrix [i] = self.adj_matrix [i] [:]

return p

```
def _get _ legal _ moves (self)
row, col = self . find(0)
free = []
```

Find which pieces can move there if row is bigger than 0.

```
Free . append (( row - 1, col ))
Free . append (( row, col – 1 ))
Free . append (( row + 1, col ))
Free . append (( row, col + 1 ))
def _ generate _ moves(self)
free = self._ get _ legal _ moves ()
zero = self . find (0)
def swap _ and _ clone (a, b)
p = self . _ clone ()
p . swap (a , b)
p. _ depth = self . _depth + 1
p. _ parent = self
return p
```

```
return map (lambda pair: swap _ and _ clone (zero, pair), free)

def _ generate _ solution _ path (self, path)

self. _ parent = = None

path . append(self)

return self. _ parent. _ generate _ solution _ path (path)

def solve(self, h)

def is_solved (puzzle)

return puzzle . adj _ matrix == _ goal _ state

openl = [self]

closedl = []

move _ count = 0

len(openl) > 0:

x = openl . pop (0)

move _ count += 1

len ( closed ) > 0

return x. _ generate _ solution _ path([])

return [ x ]

succ = x. _ generate _ moves()
```

idx _ open = idx _ closed = -1

idx _ open = index ( move, openl )

idx _ closed = index ( move, closed ) hval = h (move) fval = hval + move. _ depth

idx _ open == -1:

idx _ open > -1: copy = openl [idx _ open]

hval + copy. _ depth

hval = hval copy. _ parent = move. _ parent

copy. _ depth = move. _ depth

elif idx _ closed > -1

copy = closed [ idx _ closed]

move. _ hval = hval

closedl . remove (copy)

openl . append (move)

closedl . append (x)

openl = sorted ( openl, key=lambda p: p._hval + p. _ depth)

return [], 0

## Support Vector Machines

In artificial intelligence and machine learning, SVM's or support vector machines are common supervised learning models with different associated learning algorithms which analyze data notably used for regression and classification analysis. If you have a set of various training examples and each of them is marked as belonging to a single or to the other two categories, a support vector machine training algorithm will build a new model notably assigning some new examples to that category while making it binary linear classifier.

Every SVM model in a probabilistic classification setting is a representation of these examples commonly presented as certain points in space that are further mapped so that the different examples of these separate categories are divided by some clear gap specifically as wide as possible. Further, new examples are mapped into a certain space as well as predicted to belong to a particular category notably based on which side of the gap the examples fall. In addition to commonly performing linear classification, support vector machines may efficiently perform a non-linear classification when using what is called the kernel trick, so they are mapping a total number of their inputs into some high-dimensional feature spaces.

In the case when you have data specifically data not labeled, supervised learning will not be possible, so you have to perform an unsupervised learning that commonly attempts to find some natural clustering of the data collections, and then further map obtained data in order to find formed collections of this data. The clustering algorithm provides a greater improvement to the SVMs, so we refer to them as support vector clustering especially used in several industrial applications specifically when you have data specifically not labeled or when only some parts of the data are labeled for the further preprocessing pass.

When it comes to the implementing support vector machines in Python, we will use scikit-learns specifically widely used library when it comes to the implementing different AI projects. Fortunately, support vector machines are also available in this Python library, so you will follow the same structure like in the code presented below.

from sklearn import svm

model = svm . svc ( kernel='linear', c=1, gamma=1 )

model . fit ( X, y )

model . score ( X, y )

model . predict ( x _ test )

The following step is to tune parameters of support vector machine which will effectively improve the overall model performance. If you have a linear kernel you will need the code listing from the below.

Sklearn . svm . SVC (C=1.0, kernel='rbf', degree=3, gamma=0.0, coef0=0.0, shrinking = True

probability = False,

tol= 0.001, cache _ size=200,

class _ weight = None,

verbose = False,

max _ iter =-1,

random _ state = None)

import numpy as np

import matplotlib . pyplot as plt

from sklearn import svm, datasets

iris = datasets . load _ iris ()

```
X = iris . data [:, :2]

y = iris . target

C = 1.0

Svm . SVC ( kernel = 'linear', C=1, gamma=0 )

.fit( X, y ) x _ min,

X _ max = X [:, 0] .min() - 1, X [:, 0] .max() + 1 y _ min, y _ max = X [:, 1].min() - 1, X [:, 1]. max() + 1

h = (x _ max / x _ min)/ 100 xx,

yy = np . meshgrid (np . arrange ( x _ min, x _ max, h ),

np . arange (y _ min, y _ max, h)) plt . subplot (1, 1, 1)

Z = svc . predict ( np.c_[xx . ravel(), yy . ravel()]) Z =

Z . reshape (xx . shape)

Plt . contourf ( xx, yy, Z, cmap = plt . cm . Paired, alpha=0.8 )

plt . scatter ( X[:, 0], X[:, 1], c=y, cmap = plt . cm . Paired )

plt . xlabel ( 'Sepal length' )

plt . ylabel ( 'Sepal width' )

plt . xlim ( xx . min (), xx . max ())

plt . title ( 'SVC with linear kernel' )

plt . show ()
```

## Artificial Neural Networks

Artificial neural networks are commonly known as connectionist systems notably computing different system widely inspired by the biological neural networks especially to those constituting animal brains. These systems are capable of learning as well as progressively improving performance in order to do different tasks by considering some examples but without task-specific programming. For instance, in image recognition, ANNs might easily learn how to identify images, which contain cats simply by analyzing different example images which have been manually labeled as cat images. ANNs further use these analytics results in order to identify cats in other obtained images. The ANNs are commonly used in different applications especially when it is complex to express using rule-based programming in a traditional computer algorithm.

Every artificial neural network is based on a certain collection of different connected units known as artificial neurons notably analogous to axons contained in a biological brain. Each synapse or connection between these neurons may easily transmit a certain signal to any another neuron.

The receiving neuron or postsynaptic further processes these signals and finally the signals downstream neurons notably connected to it. It should be noted that neurons may have their state commonly represented by real numbers between 0 and 1.

Synapses, as well as neurons, commonly have their weight, which varies as learning proceeds. The strength of the neurons can decrease or increase when it comes to the signal which sends neurons downstream. Neurons and synapses further may have a threshold like that if an only certain aggregate signal is above or below, the particular level downstream specific signal sent.

Commonly, neurons are organized in certain layers. It should be noted that the different neuron layer has a capability of performing different kinds of transformations when it comes to their inputs. Signals travel from the initial input to the last layer known as output, commonly after traversing these layers several times. The ultimate goal of the artificial neural networks technique is to solve different problems in the exact same way that a human brain does. Over the time, the approach focused on matching certain mental abilities, which led to deviations from biology like backpropagation. Artificial neural networks are widely used for different AI projects including tasks like social network filtering, speech recognition, computer vision, machine translation, playing vie and board games, medical diagnosis and many other fields.

The following line of code will you how to build a simple artificial neural network in Python.

from numpy import exp, array, random, dot

training _ set _ inputs = array ( [[0, 0, 1], [1, 1, 1], [1, 0, 1], [0, 1, 1]] )

training _ set _ outputs = array ( [[0, 1, 1, 0]] ). T

random . seed (1) synaptic _ weights = 2 * random . random ( (3, 1) ) - 1

output = 1 / (1 + exp (- (dot( training _ set _ inputs, synaptic _ weights ))))

synaptic _ weights += dot(training _ set _ inputs . T, (training _ set _ outputs - output)

print 1 / (1 + exp (- ( dot(array ([1, 0, 0]), synaptic _ weights ))))

## Markov Decision Process

Markov decision process or simply MDP provides a certain mathematical framework when it comes to the modeling decision making in a different situation when you have outcomes notably partly random and partly under the decision maker control. Markov decision process is commonly used when you are studying a wide range of different optimization problems commonly solved by reinforcement learning and dynamic programming.

MDPs have been used since the 1950s and the approach was introduced by Bellman in 1957 where he conducted a core body research on MDPs which eventually led to publishing a book on the subject by Ronald A. Howard in 1960. When it comes to their area of use, MDPs are commonly used in different areas of AI including robotic as well as some other areas such as economics, manufacturing, and automated control.

To be more precise, A Markov Decision Process is a certain discrete time stochastic process. It should be noted that every MDP at each step is in a certain state, so decision maker can choose any action available at MDP's state. The process further responds at the next time just by moving into some new stage as well as giving the decision maker a particular corresponding reward. It should be noted that the probability of the process transmitting into new stage depends and is influenced the certain chosen actions.

In other words, the following stage is greatly influenced and depends on the current stage. The process is an extension of complex Markov chains with the difference when it comes to the number of actions available that are allowing rewards or giving motivation as well as allowing choice. It should be noted that MDP can reduce to Markov chain is only single action exist for certain stage while all rewards available are the same.

In order to implement Markov decision process in Python depending on your problem, you may need an interface in order to determine the MDP.

class MarkovDecisionProcess

def transition ( self, from _ state, action, to _ state )

raise NotImplementedError def initial _ state ( self )

raise NotImplementedError def reward ( self, state )

raise NotImplementedError def discount ( self, state )

raise NotImplementedError

You may also need the code for the modified dict class.

class SumDict ( dict )

```
def __setitem__ ( self, key, value ) self . has_key ( key)
```

```
value += self . get ( key ) dic . __setitem__ ( self, key, value )
```

After this step you are able to define the MDP.

```
import numpy as np

class ToyMDP ( MarkovDecisionProcess )

def __init__(self)

self . world = np . array ([ [ -0.04, -0.04, -0.04, 1 ],

[ -0.04, None, -0.04, -1 ],

[ -0.04, -0.04, -0.04, -0.04], ])

Self . initial _ state = (0, 0)

Self . finals = [ (0,3), (1,3) ]

Self . actions = ( 'l', 'r', 'u', 'd') def __iter__( self )

class Iterator: def __init__( self, iterator, finals )

self . iterator = iterator

self . finals = finals def next ( self )

True: coords = self . iterator . coords

val = self . iterator . next()
```

return coords, val

return Iterator (self . world . flat, self . finals)

def _move (self, state, action)

shape = self . world . shape

next = list ( state )

elif action == 'l' and \ (state[1] > 0 and self . world[state[ 0 ]] [state [1]-1 ] != None):

next [1] -= 1

d = SumDict ()

d [self. _ move (state, 'l')] = 0.8

d [self. _ move (state, 'u')] = 0.1 d [self . _ move ( state, 'd' )] = 0.1

return self . successors ( from _ state, action )[ to _ state ]

def initial _ state (self)

return self . initial _ state def reward ( self, state )

return self . world [state [0] ] [ state[1]] def discount ( self )

return 1

## Natural Language Processing

Natural language processing or simply NLP has commonly used techniques in different fields including computational linguistics, artificial intelligence and computer science mainly concerned with the different interactions between human or natural language and computers. Natural language processing I also concerned with programming computers in order to process huge natural language corpora. When it comes to the challenges in natural language processing, they commonly involve connecting language to machine perception, natural language understanding, machine-readable logical forms, dialog systems, natural language generation and others.

This technique is used in order to refer from speech recognition to certain language generation where every step requires a different natural language technique like Named Entity Recognition or Part-of-Speech tagging. In the following section, you will see how to build your own natural language processing assistant in Python. Before we get to know the software better, you should try natural language processing online. When it comes to the software, we will use Python's NLTK commonly used library notably containing a lot or already built in functions as well as a collection of text that will help you to get started with your NLP model. Before you embark on this adventure, make sure that you have NLTK library installed.

In order to begin, you will need to tokenize a certain sentence specifically enabling you to handle different individual words as well as punctuation marks within your sentence.

Tokenization

from nltk import word _ tokenize

sentence = " What is the weather in Los Angeles? "

tokens = word _ tokenize (sentence)

As soon as you have your tokens ready for the further processing, you can move to the next step of stop word removal. This step involves the removal all the words that are unnecessary and that simply do not contribute to any semantic meaning. Those are the words like an, the, and, etc. Python library NLTK already provides a collection of inbuilt stop words for eleven languages.

Removing the unbuilt NLTK stop words

from nltk . corpus import stopwords

stop _ words = set (stopwords . words(' english '))

```
clean _ tokens = [ w for w in tokens if not w in stop _ words ]

clean _ tokens [ 'What', 'weather', 'Los Angeles', '?' ]
```

One of the most essential parts when it comes to the speech recognition is speech tagging. In this stage, you are able to tag every word within a sentence as an adjective, noun, verb, etc. In order to do this, you will use NLTK function particularly those able to perform Parts of Speech tagging.

```
import nltk

tagged = nltk . pos _ tag (clean _ tokens)

tagged

[ ( 'What', 'WP' ), ( ' weather ', 'NN' ), ( ' Los Angeles ', 'NNP' ), ('?', '.')]
```

This tagged list contains different tuples of the form or word. When it comes to the next step, you will need NER or named entity recognition, which also goes by names Entity Extraction or Entity Identification. We need this step since Named Entity Recognition involves identifying every named entity.

NER further puts all named entities into different categories like the name of an organization, a location, etc. In order to perform NER, you will use NLTK function that classifies all named entities. In the following function, Parts of Speech tagging are represented as the input of the function.

Print ( nltk . ne _ chunk( tagged ))

( S What/WP weather/NN ( GPE Los Angeles/NNP ) ?/.)

After you named entity recognition, the overall meaning of the sentence is entirely analyzed, so you will make the appropriate call to you API. For example, in the sentence used here, after recognizing the location as Los Angeles, the context of weather may be made to some cloud based service. Then, the current weather will be displayed to the user who asked the question about the weather in Los Angeles. This is the code listing in order to get started with natural language processing using NLTK Python library. This technology is used in major intelligent personal assistants such as Siri, Amazon Alexa, and Google Now.

# Chapter 3 Artificial Intelligence Methodology

## Reinforcement Learning

Reinforcement learning is one of the most important questions for experts and scientist who are involved in artificial intelligence problems and projects. It is more than apparent why they desire to know these answers regarding the reinforcement learning. In they can understand these problems, they will, in fact, enable human to do things we were not able to do before. Therefore, with reinforcement learning, we will be able to train devices and machines to do more human tasks as well as to create something very close to the true artificial intelligence.

However, there is not yet a complete answer to the important question from the above, but there are things which proven to be more clear especially when it comes to the recent times. We all learn by interacting with our environment no matter what we are trying to accomplish. Whether you are learning to drive a car or whether an infant is learning to walk, in both scenarios a human will learn by noticing environment and by interacting with the environment. The foundation all many theories of learning, as well as the foundation of intelligence, are learning from the environment, and this concept is also integrated into many AI practices and researchers.

In this section of the book, we will explore reinforcement learning particularly a goal-oriented as well as based on interaction with our environment. It is said that reinforcement learning is the ultimate hope when it comes to the true artificial intelligence. I have to admit it is completely rightly said so since there is a huge potential of reinforcement learning when it comes to the limitless possibilities of machine learning. This approach is growing rapidly since it produces a wide range of different learning algorithm notably used for various applications. Therefore, it is important to get to know basic concepts of reinforcement learning if you are thinking about doing some AI research or project.

Once you are there and once you have the basic knowledge of reinforcement learning, you will understand as well as be able to implement it on your own AI project. The approach is learning what to do as well as how to map different situations to actions. The ultimate goal is to maximize that numerical reward signal. It should be noted that the learner is not told which certain action to take, but he or she must discover which action may yield that maximum reward. In order to devote to reinforcement learning, you will first observe and notice things from your environment, and then you will have your first attempt when it comes to the rewards. You have to remember that with reinforcement learning, there are many things you should keep in mind like balancing different tasks, paying attention to your environment and observing and noticing things which you will use in your AI project.

It should be noted that reinforcement learning, in fact, belongs to some bigger class of machine learning algorithms. You are already aware of the fact that machine learning involves supervised, unsupervised and reinforcement learning. Supervised is task driven including regression and classification while unsupervised in data drive or clustering. On the other hand, reinforcement learning involves algorithms, which learn to react to an environment, so you notice the difference.

In order to understand how to solve some reinforcement learning problem, you have to understand and get to know the problem of exploitation and exploration and then you are ready to embark on solving your reinforcement learning problem. In order to understand this, we should suppose that we have many slot machines which offer random payouts. We need to discover and get the maximum bonus from a slot machine as quickly as possible. A naïve approach is to select just one slot machine and keep playing on it all day long. Well, it sounds more than boring, even though there is a possibility of hitting the jackpot. This approach is commonly defined as a pure exploitation, and it is not the optimal choice.

On the other hand, there is another approach, for instance, when you play on every slot machine. This approach is also not that optimal, even there is still a possibility of hitting a jackpot. This approach is defined as pure exploration. It is more than apparent that neither of this approaches is optimal since there is no proper balance in order to get that maximum rewards. This is very common exploitation vs exploration dilemma when it comes to the reinforcement learning.

In order to get close to the reward, you have to formally define framework notably for defying a solution in any reinforcement learning scenario. It can be designed as set of states noted as S, set of actions noted as A, reward function noted as R and value V. In order to properly implement reinforcement learning you will use a Deep Q-learning algorithm notably commonly used policy mainly based on learning algorithm with some function approximator as an artificial neural network. Google commonly uses this particular algorithm in order to beat humans and its Atari games. You will initialize Q as well as choose an action. You further perform an action, measure reward and update Q.

Now, it is time to integrate that into Python and code it up. You will run the following commands.

git clone https://github.com/matthiasplappert/keras-rl.gitcd keras-rl python setup.py install

You will install different dependencies for your environment.

pip install h5py

pip install gym

Further, you will import modules, which are necessary.

import numpy as np

import gym from keras . models

import Sequential

from keras . layers import Dense, Activation, Flatten

from keras . optimizers import Adam from rl . agents.dqn import DQNAgent

from rl.policy import EpsGreedyQPolicy

from rl . memory import SequentialMemory

Then you will set all relevant variables.

ENV_NAME = 'CartPole-v0'

env = gym . make( ENV_NAME )

np . random . seed( 123 )

env . seed( 123 )

nb _ actions = env . action _ space .n

You will build hidden neural network layer

model = Sequential()

model . add (Flatten( input_shape =(1,) + env . observation _ space . shape ))

model . add ( Dense( 16 ))

model . add (Activation( 'relu' ))

```
model . add(Dense( nb _ actions ))

model . add( Activation( 'linear' )) p

rint ( model . summary ())
```

Further, you will configure as well as compile your agent.

```
policy = EpsGreedyQPolicy ()

memory = SequentialMemory ( limit=50000, window _ length=1 )

dqn = DQNAgent (model=model, nb _ actions=nb _ actions, memory=memory, nb _ steps _ warmup =10

target _ model _ update=1e-2, policy=policy)

dqn . compile (Adam( lr=1e-3), metrics=[ 'mae' ])

dqn . fit( env, nb _ steps=5000, visualize = True, verbose=2)
```

Test your reinforcement learning model. In this section, you have seen a fundamental implementation of reinforcement learning performed in Python. As soon as you figure this process, you are ready to embark on other and more challenging problems.

```
Dqn . test ( env, nb _ episodes=5, visualize=True )
```

## Regression and Classification

In this section of the book, we will explore classification and regression which are supervised learning problems. Since you are already familiar with these terms, we can jump immediately into Python coding and create classification and regression in Python. The problem solved in supervised learning like regression and classification will show you the link between the observed data and some external data which you will be trying to predict commonly called labels or target. In this section, we will use supervised estimators built in Python library scikit. These created prediction trees specialize in predicting outcomes. These models commonly work with estimation. In order to start, you will load your data.

```
from sklearn . datasets import load _ iris
iris = load _ iris ()
X, y = iris . data, iris . target
features = iris . feature _ names
```

As soon as you load your data into value X that contains a certain predictor and holds the classification, you will be able to define any cross-validation in order to check the results while using decision trees.

```
from sklearn . cross _ validation import cross _ val _ score
from sklearn . cross _ validation import KFold
crossvalidation = KFold (n=X.shape [0], n _ folds=5
shuffle= True, random _ state=1)
```

If you use the DecisionTreeClassiffier, you will be able to define a certain max-depth specifically inside an iterative loop in order to experiment. With various effects when it comes to the increasing the complexity of the final tree. The common expectation is to reach that ideal point as soon as possible and then to witness that decreasing cross-validation overall performance due to over-fitting. It should be noted that the best solution is a tree containing four splits. As soon as you are done, you can check the complexity of your resulting tree.

```
from sklearn import
tree _ classifier = tree . DecisionTreeClassifier
max _ depth=depth, random _ state=0 )
```

.fit (X,y). tree _. max _ depth

score = np . mean ( cross _ val _ score (tree _ classifier, X, y, scoring='accuracy', cv=crossvalidation, n _ jobs=1 ))

print 'Depth: %i Accuracy: %.3f' % ( depth , score )

Depth: 1 Accuracy: 0.580

Depth: 2 Accuracy: 0.913

Depth: 3 Accuracy: 0.920

Depth: 4 Accuracy: 0.940

Depth: 5 Accuracy: 0.920

## Clustering Algorithms

Clustering data is unlabeled data which may easily be a performer with the Python sklearn cluster. It should be noted that every clustering algorithm commonly comes in two different variants including a class that implements the fit function in order to learn all the clusters contained in train data, and a certain function, which returns an array of different integer labels notably corresponding to the various clusters. You will find the labels over the certain training data in the labels' attitude. In the following section, you will see K-means clustering algorithm, which will yield using three certain clusters. You will also see the effect of any bad initialization when it comes to the classification problem.

import numpy as np

import matplotlib . pyplot as plt

from sklearn . cluster import KMeans

from sklearn import datasets

np . random . seed(5) iris = datasets . load _ iris ()

X = iris . data

y = iris . target

estimators = [( 'k_means_iris_8', KMeans ( n _ clusters=8 ))

( 'k_means_iris_3', KMeans (n _ clusters=3 ))

( 'k _ means _ iris _ bad _ init', KMeans (n _ clusters=3, n _ init=1, init='random'))]

fignum = 1

titles = [ '8 clusters', '3 clusters', '3 clusters, bad initialization' ]

fig = plt . figure( fignum, figsize = ( 4, 3 ))

ax = Axes3D(fig, rect= [0, 0, .95, 1] , elev = 48, azim=134)

est . fit (X) labels = est . labels_

ax . scatter (X[:, 3], X[:, 0], X[:, 2], c=labels . astype (np.float), edgecolor = 'k')

ax . w _ xaxis . set _ ticklabels ([])

ax . w _ yaxis . set _ ticklabels ([])

ax . w _ zaxis . set _ ticklabels ([])

ax . set _ xlabel ('Petal width')

ax . set _ ylabel ('Sepal length')

ax . set _ zlabel ('Petal length')

ax . set _ title (titles[fignum - 1])

ax . dist = 12 fignum = fignum + 1

plt . figure (fignum, figsize = ( 4, 3 ))

ax = Axes3D (fig, rect = [0, 0, .95, 1], elev=48

azim = 134) for name, label in [( 'Setosa' , 0), ('Versicolour' , 1), ( 'Virginica' , 2)]

ax.text3D(X[y == label, 3]. Mean (), X[y = = label, 0]. Mean (), X[y = = label, 2].mean() + 2, name

horizontalalignment = 'center', bbox = dict ( alpha=.2, edgecolor ='w', facecolor='w' ))

np . choose (y, [1, 2, 0]) . astype(np.float)

ax . scatter ( X[:, 3], X[:, 0], X[:, 2 ], c=y, edgecolor= 'k' )

ax . w _ xaxis . set _ ticklabels ([])

61

```
ax.w_yaxis.set_ticklabels([])
ax.w_zaxis.set_ticklabels([])
ax.set_xlabel('Petal width')
ax.set_ylabel('Sepal length')
ax.set_zlabel('Petal length')
ax.set_title('Ground Truth')
ax.dist = 12
fig.show()
```

# Chapter 4 Build a Recommender Systems

In this chapter, we will see how to build a recommender system using Python. It should be noted at the very beginning that recommendation systems are just an automated form of any other system. These systems are commonly used in a form of a shop counter guy when well-trained system sell you products in cross selling.

These systems have the ability to recommend some personalized content notably based on past behavior. It, in fact, brings customer delight as well as gives them a reason in order to keep returning to the product or brand. You can ask the system which product you may buy, and it will show you recommended products for you based on your pars behavior and past purchases.

In the following section, you will see how can you create your own recommender system using Python and GraphLab. Before embarking on this adventure, you should know that there are different types of recommender systems like those where there is no any personalization involved or those systems which use a classifier in order to make a certain recommendation.

The system which uses a classifier incorporates personalization and it works even in the cases when the user's history of purchases is short or even not available at all.

The third type or recommender system is known as recommendation algorithm especially tailor-made in order to solve different recommendation system problems including two most typical kinds, Collaborative Filtering and Content Based. In this section, we will use the MovieLens for building our recommendation system.

You will need to download dataset in order to begin. It consists of 100,000 rating from more than thousand users on more than two thousand movies. In order to start, you will load downloaded data into Python.

import pandas as pd

u_cols = [ 'user _ id', 'age', 'sex', 'occupation', 'zip_code' ]

users = pd . read _ csv('ml-100k/u.user', sep='|', names=u _ cols,

encoding= 'latin-1')

r_cols = [ 'user_id', 'movie_id', 'rating', 'unix_timestamp' ]

```
ratings = pd . read _ csv ( 'ml-100k/u.data', sep='\t',
names=r _ cols
```

```
encoding= 'latin-1' )
```

```
i_cols = [ 'movie id', 'movie title' ,'release date','video
release date', 'IMDb URL', 'unknown', 'Action',
'Adventure', 'Animation', 'Children\'s', 'Comedy', 'Crime',
'Documentary', 'Drama', 'Fantasy', 'Film-Noir', 'Horror',
'Musical', 'Mystery', 'Romance', 'Sci-Fi', 'Thriller', 'War',
'Western']
```

```
items = pd . read _ csv ('ml-100k/u.item', sep='|'
```

```
names=i _ cols
```

```
encoding= 'latin-1')
```

You will notice that there are exactly 943 users and you have five features for their unique ID, gender, occupation as well as the zip code of their location. You will see movies rating as well.

You will also notice that there are 100K movie ratings for various users including different movies combinations. You will also notice a certain timestamp particularly associated with every user.

```
print ratings . shape ratings.head ()
print items . shape items . head ()
```

This certain data contains 1682 movies and there are twenty-four columns with specific movie genre. You will divide the rating into train and test data for further models.

R _ cols = [ 'user_id', 'movie_id', 'rating', 'unix_timestamp' ]

ratings _ base = pd . read _ csv ('ml-100k/ua.base', sep='\t'

names = r _ cols, encoding = 'latin-1' ) ratings _ test = pd . read_csv ( 'ml-100k/ua.test', sep='\t', names=r_cols, encoding='latin-1' )

ratings _ base . shape

ratings _ test . shape

Output: (( 90570, 4 ), ( 9430, 4 ))

As soon as you done, you will be able to use this obtained data for both testing and training. You will be able to make any content based system as well as collaborative filtering algorithm using this model.

## Automatic Speech Recognition

In this section of the book, you will get to know better an excellent Google Speech Recognition API. This certain API converts text into written text. You will be able to simply speak and Google API will easily convert it into text and you will get excellent results written in English. Google also has created JavaScript, so you will be able to recognize your speech in Java if you like.

In order to start, you have to install packages including PyAudio, speech recognition, and PortAudio. It should be noted that PyAudio version 0.2.9. is also required and there is a strong possibility that you will have to complete the survey manually.

git clone

cd pyaudio sudo python setup . py install

sudo apt - get installl libportaudio - dev

sudo apt - get install python-dev

sudo apt - get install libportaudio0 libportaudio2 libportaudiocpp0 portaudio19 -dev

sudo pip3 install SpeechRecognition

As soon as you install the program, it will record audio coming from your microphone and it will send the certain speech API as well as return a Python string. The audio is recorded via the speech recognition module and the module is also included on the top of the program. Further, you will send your speech to the API which will return the output.

```
import speech _ recognition as sr

r = sr. Recognizer () with sr . Microphone () as source

print ("Say!")

audio = r . listen (source)

print ( "You said: " + r.recognize _ google ( audio ))

print ( "Google Speech Recognition could not understand audio" )

print ( "Could not request results from Google Speech Recognition service; {0}". format ( e ))
```

# Chapter 5 Genetic and Logic Programming

Genetic and logic programming are commonly used techniques when it comes to the artificial intelligence tasks. When it comes to the genetic programming, the technique is used as a collection of genes which are modified or evolved using a certain evolutionary algorithm known as GA. It is an application of different algorithms in which space of solutions is composed of various computer programs.

The results of this approach are complex computer programs which have the capability of performing well in almost every predefined task. The method is commonly used when it comes to the encoding a computer program in any artificial intelligence chromosome. This method also leads to an evaluation of its fitness in addition to possessing a certain respect towards that predefined task which is the main concept in the GP technique. It should be noted that this technique is still a very active subject of research.

On the other hand, logic programming is a certain type of programming paradigm specifically mainly based on certain formal logic. It should be noted that any program notably written in a logic programming language is a collection of a certain sentence in logical form. Sentences written in a logical programming manner also express rules as well as fact about some problem domain. Some of the major logic programming language families include Datalog, Prolog and Answer set programming or ASP. It should be noted that in this language, all rules are written in the certain form of clauses that are read declaratively like logical implications.

When it comes to the logical programming, rules, as well as fact, have no body, so they are written in the simplified form. The simplest form is known as atomic formulae where all clauses are called Horn clauses or definite clauses. However, there are many extensions when it comes to these simplified clauses. Logic programming languages include extensions, so they also that knowledge needed when it comes to the exploring the capabilities of a non-monotonic logic. In the following section, we will see how to create logic and genetic algorithms using Python. In the followings section, genetic programming meets Python so you will how to easily fight syntax trees by implementing genetic programming in Python. The following codes are implemented in pure Python. The genetic programming code is very flexible since it compiles different GP trees in built-in Python bytecodes so the function has the great speed when it comes to the execution. You will be able to use different Python objects like terminals as well as any Python expression. It should be noted that any available Python function may be used as well. You will use Python functions that will be automatically detected by the certain framework.

from pyevolve import

import math

error _ accum = Util . ErrorAccumulator ()

def gp _ add (a, b) : return a+b

def gp _ sub(a, b): return a-b def gp _ mul (a, b): return a*b

def gp _ sqrt(a): return math . sqrt ( abs ( a )) def eval _ func (chromosome)

global error _ accum error _ accum . reset ()

code _ comp = chromosome . getCompiledCode () for a in xrange (0, 5)

xrange (0, 5)

eval (code _ comp)

target = math . sqrt (( a*a )+( b*b ))

error _ accum += ( target, evaluated )

```
return error _ accum . getRMSE () def main _ run ():
genome = GTree.GTreeGP()

genome . setParams(max _ depth=5, method= "ramped" )

genome . evaluator.set( eval _ func )

ga = GsimpleGA . GsimpleGA (genome)

ga . setParams(gp _ terminals = ['a', 'b'],
gp_function_prefix = "gp")

ga . setGenerations (1000) ga . setMutationRate(0.08)
ga.setCrossoverRate(1.0)

ga . setPopulationSize (2000) ga .evolve(freq_stats=5) print
ga.bestIndividual()
```

As you can notice in the source-code, you will not need to bind different variable when you are calling the syntax tree of a different individual. You will simply use the code get compiled code approach that returns the Python certain compiled function to that stage where it is ready to be executed. It should be noted that the visualization is very flexible as well, especially if you use Python decorators in order to see how different function may be graphically represented. You may have different as well as very interesting visualization patterns thanks to changing the function gp_add.

Gtree . gpdec ( representation="+", color="red" )

def gp _ add (a, b): return a+b

Now it is the time to see how to implement logic programming approach using Python for solving a certain problem. It should be noted that logic programming is a specific general programming paradigm. Logic programming paradigm commonly came about very specifically in order to serve as widely used algorithmic core when it comes to the Computer Algebra Systems in Python. Logic paradigm also came commonly for the automated optimization and generation of numerous numeric software. The hot topics when it comes to the Python Scientific community are most certainly domain specific languages, compilers and code generation. In the following section, we will use LogPy that aims to be a low-kevel core for various projects including logic programming in AI research.

We will use LogPy which enables the expression of different relation as wekll as the search for different values that satisfy them. It should be noted that multiple variables as well as multiple goals may be used at the same tim.

```
from logpy import run, eq, membero, var, conde

x = var ()

run (1, x, eq(x, 5)) (5,)

z = var ()

run (1, x, eq(x, z), eq (z, 3)) (3,)

run (1, x, eq ((1, 2), (1, x))) (2,)

run (2, x, membero (x, (1, 2, 3)
```

It should be noted that LogPy stores different data like facts which state different relationships existing between different terms. The code form the below creates a certain parent relationship as well as uses it to state different facts about Simpsons family parents.

```
from logpy import Relation, facts

parent = Relation ()

facts (parent, ( "Homer", "Bart" ), ... ( "Homer", "Lisa "),
... ( "Abe", "Homer" ))

run (1, x, parent ( x, "Bart")) ('Homer',)

run (2, x, parent ("Homer", x)) ('Lisa', 'Bart')
```

You are also able to use different intermediate variables as well when it comes to some more complex queries. You also can express the relationship with the grandfather separately.

y = var ()

run ( 1, x, parent (x, y), parent (y, 'Bart')) ('Abe')

def grandparent (x, z): ... y = var() ... return conde((parent (x, y), parent (y, z)))

run ( 1, x, grandparent( x, 'Bart' )) ( 'Abe,' )

It should be noted that LogPy mainly depends on tuples, functions, generators, and dicts. It should be very simple when it comes to the integrating into some preexisting code since there are no new data structures or classes in LogPy.

# Conclusion

We have come to the end of the book. I am sure that by now, you are familiar with different artificial intelligence approaches as well as different techniques used when it comes to the solving common as well as more complex AI problems. The book will help you when you are ready to embark on the adventure called AI and it will most certainly help you to better understand what is the machine intelligence. AI is intelligence commonly exhibited by devices and machines rather than humans. The field of artificial intelligence is defined as the study of different intelligent agents, and today it would be almost impossible to imagine the world without AI approach and techniques.

By now you now that intelligent agents are any device or machine with the capability of perceiving its environment as well as taking certain actions when it comes to the maximizing its chance of success as some certain goal. Artificial intelligence is also applied when a device or machine mimics different cognitive functions of humans. This concept is what artificial intelligence is all about. When it comes to the different applications of AI methods, I have to mention health care, video games, finance, automotive industry and much more. Try to imagine these different fields without AI approach. Yes, it is hard since we are used to AI to be present in our environment, but we simply do not pay attention to the great significance of this relatively young field of machine learning.

It is not easy being human in this age that is completely the age of artificial intelligence, but we have to accept it as well as to take advantage of it since we can greatly benefit and enhance our lifestyle. Machine learning, as well as artificial intelligence, have become mainstream tools, especially in recent times. These techniques are being applied across numerous industries in order t0 increase profits, save lives reduce costs and improve the overall customer experience. It is important to understand and get to know different AI tools and techniques, since you may benefit greatly whether you have your own business, or you simply want to explore AI by yourself in your free time.

# Reinforcement Learning with Python

A Short Overview of Reinforcement Learning with Python

*By Anthony S. Williams*

© Copyright 2017 by Anthony S. Williams - All rights reserved.

Respective authors own all copyrights not held by the publisher.

The following publication is reproduced below with the goal of providing information that is as accurate and reliable as possible. Regardless, purchasing this publication can be seen as consent to the fact that both the publisher and the author of this book are in no way experts on the topics discussed within and that any recommendations or suggestions that are made herein are for informational purposes only. Professionals should be consulted as needed prior to undertaking any of the action endorsed herein.

This declaration is deemed fair and valid by both the American Bar Association and the Committee of Publishers Association and is legally binding throughout the United States.

Furthermore, the transmission, duplication or reproduction of any of the following work including specific information will be considered an illegal act irrespective of if it is done electronically or in print. This extends to creating a secondary or tertiary copy of the work or a recorded copy and is only allowed with express written consent from the Publisher. All additional right reserved.

The information in the following pages is broadly considered to be a truthful and accurate account of facts and as such any inattention, use or misuse of the information in question by the reader will render any resulting actions solely under their purview. There are no scenarios in which the publisher or the original author of this work can be in any fashion deemed liable for any hardship or damages that may befall them after undertaking information described herein.

Additionally, the information in the following pages is intended only for informational purposes and should thus be thought of as universal. As befitting its nature, it is presented without assurance regarding its prolonged validity or interim quality. Trademarks that are mentioned are done without written consent and can in no way be considered an endorsement from the trademark holder.

The trademarks that are used are without any consent, and the publication of the trademark is without permission or backing by the trademark owner. All trademarks and brands within this book are for clarifying purposes only and are the owned by the owners themselves, not affiliated with this document.

# Table of Contents

Introduction ................................................................... 1

**Chapter 1 Types of Machine Learning Algorithms ..... 8**

    Supervised Learning ............................................. 11

    Unsupervised Learning ........................................ 13

    Semi-Supervised Learning ................................... 15

    Reinforcement Learning ...................................... 16

**Chapter 2 Elements of Reinforcement Learning ...... 19**

**Chapter 3 Markov Decision Processes ...................... 32**

    Markov Decision Processes Parameters ........... 38

**Chapter 4 Approximate Dynamic Programming ...... 48**

    Policy Evaluation ................................................. 51

    Policy Iteration .................................................... 54

    Value Iteration .................................................... 59

**Chapter 5 Integrating with OpenAI Gym ................. 63**

    Q-Learning Algorithms ....................................... 71

**Chapter 6 Monte Carlo Methods .............................. 80**

    Monte Carlo Prediction ...................................... 81

    Monte Carlo Tree Search .................................... 85

**Chapter 7 Temporal Difference Learning ................. 88**

**Conclusion ................................................................. 93**

# Introduction

Reinforcement learning is the fundamental problem when it comes to the getting an agent to act out there in the world in a certain manner of maximizing its rewards. For instance, consider a teaching job when you are teaching your dog a certain new trick. In this case, you are not sure and you cannot tell your dog what to do, but there is an option to reward it if it does the wrong or right thing. The dog, in this case, has to figure out what it is supposed to do in order to make it to the reward. The dog also has to learn what made him deserve that punishment as well. This is known as the credit assignment issue.

Remember this example with the dog and teaching it to perform new tricks since we can use the very similar method in order to train computers to perform different tasks, like playing chess or backgammon, scheduling our jobs and meetings as well as controlling robot limbs and much more. We are able to formalize the reinforcement problem as the certain environment specifically modeled as a certain stochastic finite state device or machine with particular inputs. These inputs are, in fact, certain actions sent from the specific agent. Machines also come with certain outputs as well notably rewards and observations specifically sent to the agent. We can represent it as follows:

- State transition function is represented as $P(X(t) \mid X(t-1), A(t))$
- Observation (output) function P is represented as $(Y(t) \mid X(t), A(t))$
- Reward function is represented as $E(R(t) \mid X(t), A(t)$

You can easily notice that what certain agent sees greatly depends on what it performs. In other words, it greatly reflects the fact that certain perception is an entirely active process. It should be noted that the agent is also modeled as stochastic FSM notably containing inputs including rewards and observations specifically sent from the environment. The agent also comes with certain outputs like certain action sent to the specific environment. When it comes to the ultimate goal of the agent, is to find that policy or state-update function that will be leading it to the maximizing the expected sum of different discounted rewards. We can represent it as follows:

$$E[R_0 + gR_1 + g^2 R_2 + ...] = E \sum_{t=0}^{\infty} \gamma^t R_t$$

In this function, gamma is a certain discount factor that models that fact future reward notably less than certain immediate reward. Mathematically speaking, we need gamma to be less than one in order to make that infinite sum coverage. On the other hand, the environment will have zero rewards when it comes to its absorbing states.

Reinforcement is an area of a wide field of machine learning notably inspired by behaviorist psychology specifically concerned with how certain software agents might take different actions in a wide diversity of environments in order to maximize that notion particularly leading towards the cumulative reward. The main problem is studied in different other disciplines, including operations research, control theory, game theory, simulation-based optimization, information theory, swarm intelligence, genetic algorithms, and statistics. This greatly speaks about a wide range of reinforcement learning applications when it comes to the different scientific fields.

In the control literature and operations research, approximate dynamic programming are those fields where different reinforcement learning techniques are incorporated and carefully studied. Reinforcement learning problems also have been studied in other scientific fields like a theory of optimal controls. It should be noted that most studies are commonly concerned with the various optimal solutions and their existence in addition to their characterization rather than being concerned with the learning and different approximation aspects. In game theory and economics, reinforcement learning is commonly used in order to explain how equilibrium can arise under certain bounded rationality.

When it comes to the machine learning, the environment is commonly formulated as a certain MDP also known as Markov decision process as different reinforcement learning practices and algorithms for this context commonly utilized various dynamic programming methods and techniques. When it comes to the main difference between reinforcement learning and other classical algorithms, I have to mention the one regarding the latter that do not need any knowledge on MDP and they still target huge MDPs where some more exact methods simply become invisible.

Reinforcement learning greatly differs from other standard supervised learning techniques since reinforcement algorithms correct output and input pairs, but never present them. It should be noted that sum-optima actions are never explicitly corrected and presented as well. Reinforcement learning algorithms instead focus mainly on on-line performance that involves finding that balance between exploitation and exploration. In these terms, exploitation is that current knowledge while exploration is a certain uncharted territory. There is a common reinforcement method or exploration vs. exploitation relationship notably studies through common multi-armed bandit problem as well as in different finite MDPs.

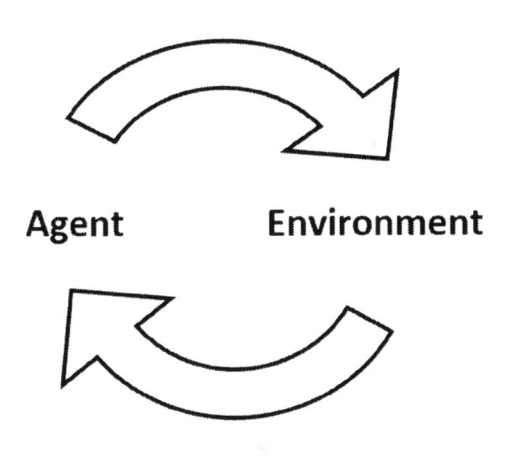

**Agent**     **Environment**

Reinforcement learning is commonly used practice when it comes to the machine learning. It allows machines and software agents to automatically determine the specific ideal behavior within a particular context in order to maximize its performance. Reinforcement learning is greatly concerned with the common problem of finding the most suitable actions to take in a specific situation to maximize the most suitable reward. It should be noted that reinforcement learning algorithms are not given any specific goal. These algorithms instead are mainly forced to learn their optimal goals by error and trial.

You can think of the classic game Mario Bros. In this game, different reinforcement algorithms would learn by error and trial and determine that specific movements, as well as the button, push notably advancing the player's standing and players' score in the game. In this case, error and trial aim in order to result in a certain optimal state when it comes to the gameplay. The reinforcement learning algorithm also prophesies that interaction existing between the learning agent and environment. The environment commonly rewards the agent for any corrective action particularly the reinforcement signal. Leveraging the certain rewards obtained, further, the agent improves its particular environments knowledge in order to select the following action.

Reinforcement learning when it comes to the artificial intelligence is a certain kind of dynamic programming which, trains different algorithms mainly using a system of punishment and reward. A reinforcement learning agent or algorithm learns everything relevant by interacting with its certain environment. The reinforcement learning agent receives a particular reward by performing in a current manner and it receives penalties when performing in an incorrect manner. It should be noted that the algorithm or agent is able to learn from its environment without any intervention from human by minimizing its penalty and maximizing its reward.

Reinforcement learning is a commonly used approach to machine learning which is absolutely inspired by behaviorist psychology. You can think of the approach in a similar manner to how a child embarks on an adventure and new state in life when trying to walk or when trying to perform any new task. It should be noted that this approach contrasts other learning approaches in that reinforcement algorithm is not told hor to perform a certain task. The algorithm works through the issues completely on its own.

# Chapter 1 Types of Machine Learning Algorithms

In this section of the book, you will get to know the differences between reinforcement learning and other types of machine learning algorithms. It is more than apparent that we are living in this most defining period when it comes to the human history. This the period when computing rapidly moved from certain large mainframes to desktop computers than finally to the cloud. However, what makes ti certain period the most defining, in fact, is something that has not happened yet, but it is clearly coming our way in these several years to come.

What makes this certain period exciting for someone like us, is the great democratization of the techniques and tools that followed this great boost in computing. Today, data scientists are able to build an amazing data-crunching machine with some complex algorithms in just a few hours, and that is what makes this period the most defining in the human history. However, reaching to this point in data science was not easy, and like many other periods, this period as well had some very dark nights and days.

In this section of the book, you will understand common types of machine learning algorithms compared to the subject of the book, reinforcement learning. There are three types of machine learning algorithms including supervised learning, unsupervised learning and reinforcement learning. In order to better understand the main concept behind the reinforcement learning, you have to get to know other machine learning types briefly, before we embark on serious machine learning in Python.

Machine learning comes in different flavors that depend on the algorithm or model and its overall objectives. The types of machine learning algorithms are divided into these three groups based on their purpose. It is very useful to tour different machine learning algorithms so you can devote to reinforcement learning with a basic understanding of supervised and unsupervised learning techniques.

These learning techniques are commonly grouped by the learning style and by similarity. Some of the most common learning techniques grouped by their similarity are regression algorithms, regularization algorithms, instance-based algorithms, Bayesian algorithms, Decision tree algorithms and Artificial neural network algorithms. In the following section, you will be introduced to these most common machine learning algorithms and their purpose. Think of them as representative notably very useful since you will get an idea of machine learning fundamentals that will come useful when it comes to the reinforcement learning algorithms.

| Types of Machine Learning Algorithms |||
|---|---|---|
| **Supervised Learning** | **Unsupervised Learning** | **Reinforcement Learning** |
| Makes machines learn explicitly | Machine understands the data and identifies structures | An approach to artificial intelligence |
| Data with clearly defined data is given | Evaluation is qualitative or indirect | Reward based learning |
| Direct feedback is given | Does not predict or find anything specific | Machine learns how to act in a certain environment |
| Predicts outcomes | | Maximizing rewards and minimizing penalties |
| Resolves classification and regression problems | | |

## Supervised Learning

In this section, I am focused on explaining to you machine learning algorithms notably grouped by their learning style. There are many different ways when it comes to the training machine learning model. The algorithm also can model different problems mainly based on its interaction with the environment or experience. We will first have a look at supervised machine learning. In this certain approach, input data is commonly called as training data and it has an already known label and result like not-spam or spam or certain stock price at a certain time. A supervised learning model is prepared through the careful training process in which it is mandatory to make a certain prediction. The model is further corrected by this prediction that turned out to be wrong. The training process then continues until the algorithm achieves that desired level of accuracy when it comes to the training data. Most common supervised algorithms are regression and classification including Back Propagation Neural Network and Logistic Regression.

When it comes to the supervised learning approach, we have a certain model consisting of outcome variables and target variables. Outcomes variable is also known as a dependent variable specifically predicted from a certain given set of different predictors also known as independent variables. Using these variables, we are able to generate a function notably able of mapping inputs to every desired output. The training process than continues.

Supervised learning happens when a model learns from certain exampled data and when a model is associated with certain target responses which can consist of string labels like classes and tags or numeric value. To later predict that correct response when posed with some new examples, the model will obtain certain numeric values or string labels. The supervised approach is very similar to human learning under some kind of supervision like a teacher or like a parent. The teacher or parent provides to students and children some good examples needed to be remembered by children. Further, child or student is able to derive some general rules when it comes to these specific examples.

It should be noted that regression problems target certain numeric values, while classification problems target some qualitative variable like tag or class. A regression task mainly determines that average prices of houses located in Los Angeles, and classification problem may distinguish different types of flows based on their petal and sepal measures.

## Unsupervised Learning

When it comes to the unsupervised machine learning algorithms, we do not have any outcome or target variable to estimate or predict. This technique is used mainly for clustering population when it comes to the different groups. The technique is also widely used for segmenting customers in certain groups for particular intervention. Common unsupervised algorithms include K-means and Apriori algorithm. Unsupervised learning occurs when a model or algorithms learn from certain plain examples with no any associated response. It means that the technique leads to the model notably determine by itself the certain data patterns. This type of algorithm also tends to completely restructure the data into something completely different like some new features commonly representing a new series of different uncorrelated values or some new class. These models are of great significance when it comes to the providing humans with valuable insight into the overall meaning of data and providing assistance when it comes to the relevant and useful inputs to other models like supervised learning algorithms.

This learning approach greatly resembles the methods which humans use in order to figure out some certain events or objects within the same class, commonly by observing that degree of similarity existing between objects. A wide range of recommendation system which you can find on the web like marketing automation is mainly based on unsupervised learning techniques. The marketing automation model is able of deriving its suggestion based on your purchase history on based on that what you have bought in the past. These recommendation systems are mainly based on a certain estimation of what group of loyal customers you resemble the most. This system then by inferring your most likely preferences based on that obtained group of customers.

When it comes to the unsupervised learning, certain input data does not have any known result and it is not labeled. An unsupervised algorithm is prepared by firstly deducing certain structures notably present within the input data. This occurs in order to be able to extract some general rules. It may be done by a certain mathematical process in order to systematically reduce that redundancy. The another approach used commonly is to organize data obtained based on similarity. Example unsupervised problems include dimensionality reduction, clustering and association rule learning.

## Semi-Supervised Learning

When it comes to the most common machine learning algorithms, I have to mention semi-supervised learning algorithms. In this particular approach, input data represents a certain mixture of some unlabelled examples in addition to labeled examples. In this approach, there is that desired prediction problem, but the algorithm first must learn the structures in order to organize data and to make predictions. Regression and classification can be semi-supervised. Semi-supervised learning algorithms are, in fact, extensions to some other flexible methods notably making an assumption about how to deal with and model the unlabeled data.

When it comes to the crunching data to model different business decision, you will use unsupervised and supervised learning methods. On the other hand, a hot topic, especially in recent times, is semi-supervised learning method when it comes to the different areas like image classification where you have those large datasets commonly containing a very small number of labeled examples.

# Reinforcement Learning

This book revolves around the third type of machine learning reinforcement learning which occurs when you have the model containing examples that lack labels, just like unsupervised learning. On the other hand, you are able to accompany any example with some negative or positive feedback in accordance with the solution notably proposed by the algorithm. This technique is commonly connected to different applications when it comes to the making certain decisions by the models. In other words, the product is entirely prescriptive in addition to being descriptive like in unsupervised learning. It should be noted that all decision bear certain consequences. In our human world, it is just like learning new things by error and trial.

In the human world, errors can help us learn because every error has a certain penalty added like loss of time, cost, pain or regret. Errors are teaching us that a specific course of our actions is less likely to turn to success than some other actions. One of the most interesting reinforcements learning models are those integrated into computers which learn to play complex video games with no human intervention. In this particular case, an application presents the model with different examples of several situations, like that situation when a gamer is stuck in a maze due to avoiding an enemy. The application further lets the model know the result of actions notably needed in order to avoid a dangerous situation and avoid an enemy.

When it comes to the reinforcement learning used in video games, applications can learn and discover situation leading to danger and pursue survival. If you are interested in video games and incorporation of reinforcement learning in games, you can have a look at how the leading company in the world, Google DeepMind was able to create a certain reinforcement learning program especially able to play by itself Atari's video games. If you decide to watch the program, you will notice that it is very clumsy at the beginning as well as very unskilled. However, the program is able to steadily improves with more training until eventually, it becomes a champion in the game.

Reinforcement learning approach uses the machine notably trained in order to make a certain decision. It commonly works in the way when the certain machine is exposed to a certain environment where it is able to trains itself continually only using error and trial. This machine further is able to learn from its past experience and it tries to capture that best possible knowledge in order to make the most accurate business decisions. Reinforcement learning is a certain decision process, specific reward system, and recommendation system.

The most common reinforcement learning algorithm is Markov Decision Process which will be explained later in the book. On the other hand, commonly used supervised and unsupervised learning algorithms used include Linear Regression, Logistic Regression, Naive Bayes, Support Vector Machines, Decision Tree, K-Means, Random Forest, KNN, Dimensionality Reduction Algorithms and Gradient Boosting Algorithms like GBM, XGBoost, CatBoost, and LightBoost. However, here we are interested in reinforcement learning and some common reinforcement learning algorithms notably explained in the following chapters. Since you are familiar with common machine learning techniques, it is time to get to know fundamentals of reinforcement learning before we dive into some practical examples of reinforcement learning with Python.

# Chapter 2 Elements of Reinforcement Learning

Reinforcement learning is learning about what to or how to map different situations to actions in such a manner to maximize that numeric reward signals. It should be noted that the learning is no told what specifically to do, what to perform and what action to take like in the other machine learning techniques, but instead, it is supposed to discover by itself which actions will most likely yield the most reward.

That idea we were able to learn by interacting with the environment is first to occur to everyone notably when we think about the overall nature and fundamentals of a learning process. Reinforcement learning is very similar to actions when a child learns how to walk when a child waves its arms. In this case, the child has no any explicit teacher, but it does have that direct sensorimotor connection to things and humans in his environment. It should be noted that exercising this environmental connection produces relevant information about the effect and cause as well as about different consequences of different actions. These connections also tell what to do when it comes to the achieving different goals.

Interactions with the environment are undoubtedly a major source of valuable knowledge, about ourselves and about our environment. We are aware of how our environment responds to certain actions performed by us. We further seek in order to influence what occurs through our certain behavior. The foundational idea notably lying nearly all machine learning theories is learning from an interaction. In this book, we simply explore and discover different reinforcement learning techniques and learning from interaction. We will also explore some idealized learning situations as well as evaluate the overall effectiveness of different reinforcement learning techniques.

In most challenging as well as most interesting cases, different actions may affect both the following situations and immediate reward. By doing so, actions are all of affecting all subsequent rewards as well. These characteristics are error and trial search and some delayed reward. It should be noted that all these characteristics are the most important certain distinguishing features when it comes to the reinforcement learning.

It should be noted that reinforcement learning is not defined by certain characterizing method, but it is mainly characterizing a certain learning problem. Any method or technique notably well suited when it comes to the solving problem, we will consider as a reinforcement learning technique. The basic idea lying behind any reinforcement learning problem is to simply capture those most important aspects of some real problem by facing a certain learning agent notably interacting with an environment in order to achieve a certain goal. It should be noted that such a learning agent must be able to properly sense the overall state of its environment into some certain extent. It also must be able to take different actions specifically affecting the overall state. The certain learning agent also must have a particular goal notably related to the overall state of its environment. This certain formulation is intended to focus and include three aspects, goals, aspects and sensation. These three fundamental aspects are included in their simplest forms without doing anything to them in order to trivialize them.

Reinforcement learning differs from supervised learning techniques greatly. It is the kind of machine learning technique notably studied in some most current research when it comes to the statistical pattern recognition, machine learning, and artificial neural networks. On the other hand, supervised learning techniques focus on learning from certain examples notably provided by some knowledgeable supervisor. This is very important part of machine learning, but alone this technique is not entirely adequate when it comes to the learning from certain interactions. In interactive learning like reinforcement learning, problems involved are often very impractical in order to obtain certain examples of that desired behavior which is correct as well as representative of all different situations in that the certain agent has to act and perform different tasks. In reinforcement learning, an agent simply must be able to collect valuable information by itself and learn from its environment by error and trial.

When it comes to the different challenges, which commonly arise in reinforcement learning projects, I have to mention that in this technique, learning is understood as a certain trade-off between exploitation and exploration. In order to obtain a great reward, a certain reinforcement learning agent must prefer certain actions which are has tried in its past and found to be very effective when it comes to the producing a certain reward.

In order to discover suitable actions in order to get a reward, a reinforcement learning agent has to try different actions which have not selected in its past. The agent also has to exploit information that has already know to obtain a certain reward. It also has to explore to make some better action selection in the near future while moving towards a certain reward. It should be noted that neither exploitation and exploration can be pursued without failing at some point, and that is the greatest dilemma when it comes to the reinforcement learning projects. Therefore, a certain learning agent must try different actions in order to progressively favor those which appear to be the most suitable. If we look at a certain project on a stochastic task, then every action must be tried several times in order to gain that reliable estimate of some expected reward.

The exploration-exploitation dilemma, in fact, has been intensively studied by different mathematicians in the past few decades. For now, we are sure that the entire issues when it comes to the finding that balance between exploitation and exploration does not even arise in other learning techniques like supervised learning. However, when it comes to some larger trends of that reinforcement learning is a great part towards that greater interaction and contact between different engineering disciplines and artificial intelligence. It should be noted that not that long time ago, a field of artificial intelligence was viewed as entirely separate from statistics and control theory. However, over the last decades, that view eroded.

Therefore, modern artificial intelligence approach accepts control theory as well as statistics.

Before we get to know the essentials and basic elements of reinforcement learning, the best way to understand the concepts lying under reinforcement learning is to get to know some of the most common examples and reinforcement learning applications which greatly guided the overall development of this machine learning approach. You can think of a master chess player who is about to make his move. The overall choice is informed by not anticipating possible replies as well as counterreplies and by planning different moves. The choice is also informed by some immediate as well as intuitive judgments of that great desirability of certain moves and positions.

Another great example of reinforcement learning is an adaptive controller notably label of adjusting parameters of some petroleum refinery's operation situated in real time. The controller is able of optimizing the quality trade-off on the certain basis of already specified marginal costs, but without sticking strictly to that set of points notably suggested by engineers. Another example is a gazelle calf which struggles to its feet just minutes after being born. However, half an hour later, it is able to run approximately at 20 miles per hour. In the following section, you will get to know the basic elements of reinforcement learning.

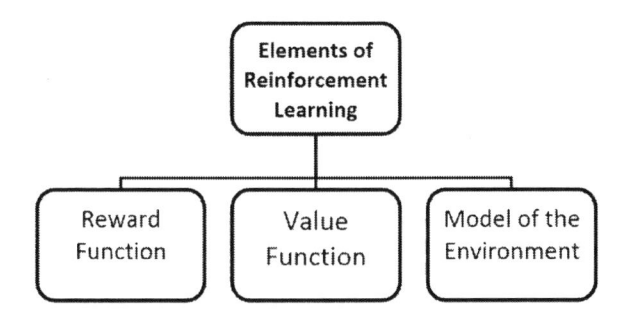

```
                    ┌─────────────────┐
                    │   Elements of   │
                    │  Reinforcement  │
                    │    Learning     │
                    └─────────────────┘
                             │
         ┌───────────────────┼───────────────────┐
  ┌─────────────┐    ┌─────────────┐    ┌─────────────┐
  │   Reward    │    │    Value    │    │ Model of the│
  │  Function   │    │   Function  │    │ Environment │
  └─────────────┘    └─────────────┘    └─────────────┘
```

Beyond the environment and the agent, one model is able to identify four other subelements of common reinforcement learning system including a reward function, a policy, and models of the environment. When it comes to the policy, it is able of defining the certain learning agent'way of specific behaviors at some given time. Generally speaking, a certain policy is a mapping from some perceived states of the certain environment to specific actions notably taken within those certain states. A policy also corresponds to what in certain psychology field would be named a set of certain stimulus-response and associations.

There are also some cases when a policy is a very simple function of some lookup table. On the other hand, in some cases, a policy may commonly involve some extensive computation like a search process. The policy is the basis of a reinforcement learning agent in that common sense when a certain agent is sufficient when it comes to the determining certain behavior. It should be noted that policies can be stochastic as well.

The common reinforcement element is also a reward function. It is able of defining that specific goal in a reinforcement learning issue. Generally speaking, a reward function is able to map every perceived state and state-action pairs of the certain environment to a single number or reward. Further, it indicates that desirability of that certain state. When it comes to the ultimate reinforcement learning objective, it is to maximize that total reward it receives in terms of a long run. The reward function also defines what are bad and what are good events for the reinforcement agent.When it comes to the biological system, it simply would not be proper to identify certain rewards with pain and pleasure since there are many immediate as well as defining features of the issue notably faced by the reinforcement agent.

It should be noted that any reward function must be unalterable by certain reinforcement agent. However, it commonly serves as a basis when it comes to the altering policies. For instance, is some action is selected by a certain policy notably followed by some low reward, that policy may be easily changed in order to select some completely other actions in that certain situation in the near future. It should be noted that reward functions also may be stochastic.

A reward function commonly indicated what is good and what is bad in some immediate sense, while a value function is able of specifying what is good, but in the long run. Generally speaking, the value of a certain state is that total amount or reward an agent may expect to accumulate over sometime in the future, starting from an initial state. Values also are able of indicating that long-term desirability of certain states especially after taking into account different states which are likely to follow as well as to reward agents available in that certain states.

In human analogy, rewards are just like pain and pleasure. Therefore, values commonly correspond to some more refined and more farsighted judgment of how displeased and pleased we are when our environment in some certain state. So, expressed in this way, we simply hope it is very clear that value function will formalize that familiar and basic idea.

It should be noted that reward in a certain sense primarily, while on the other hand, certain predictions of rewards are entirely secondary. Just remember that without rewards there would be no any values, and the main purpose is to estimate values in order to achieve more rewards. In fact, it is a value with that we are commonly most concerned when we are making and evaluating different decisions. Certain action choice is made notably based on some value judgments. We commonly seek different actions which bring some states of the highest value and not states with the highest reward since certain actions are able of obtaining that greatest amount when it comes to the rewards in terms of some longer run. In planning and decision making, that derived quantity is called value, and that is what concerns us the most.

It should be that determining values in the greater challenge than determining rewards since rewards commonly are given directly by the certain environment, while values, on the other hand, must be reestimated and estimated from certain sequences of different observations notably done by an agent noticing its environment and learning from it over its entire lifetime. It should be noted that the most important component of the majority of reinforcement learning models is a method for more efficient estimating values.

Reinforcement learning is all about observing and learning from the environment done with interacting. It is our greatest belief that those certain methods are able to take some advantage of certain details of some individual behavior interactions and that these methods are commonly much more efficient that some other evolutionary cases.

On the other hand, evolutionary methods commonly ignore that much useful structure when it comes to the common reinforcement learning problems. These methods also do not use fact that states that an individual passes through different states during its lifetime. Therefore, in many cases, the relevant and important information may be misleading when these states are misperceived.

Even though reinforcement learning and evolutionary methods have so much in common, we simply do not consider these evolutionary methods by themselves to ve well suited when it comes to the common reinforcement learning problems. The final element of reinforcement learning system in optionally a model of the environment.

A model fo the environment simply mimics that certain behavior of the environment.

- Reward function defines the ultimate goal in a reinforcement learning problem. In order to achieve this goal, a policy is altered.
- Value function: Reward function indicate what is good when it comes to the immediate sense while a value function is able of specifying what is good in the long run.
- Model of the environment: Predict and mimic the behaviors of the environment. Model of the environment is commonly used for planning is you know that current state and action. In this case, it can predict the resultant next stage as well as next reward.

As I already mentioned before, the model of the environment is able of predicting as well as mimicking the certain environment. For instance, given a certain state as well as an action, the model may be able to predict that resultant next stage as well as the next reward. These models are commonly used for planning and for anyway when it comes to the deciding on a certain course of action mainly by considering that possible future situation even before these actions actually were experienced by the reinforcement learning model.

When it comes to the incorporation of these models, I have to say that the models are something newly integrated into reinforcement learning projects. It is fair to say that these models are absolutely new development. When it comes to some early reinforcement learning systems, these were entirely trial-and-error learners. These early systems were entirely opposed to the planning methods. However, techniques have improved since it becomes clear that reinforcement learning is absolutely related to dynamic programming approach and techniques since reinforcement learning uses different models related to state-space planning methods.

# Chapter 3 Markov Decision Processes

Markov decision processes or MDPs commonly provide that mathematical framework when it comes to the modeling some decision making especially in situations where certain outcomes are partly random and partly under some control of decision maker. MDPs are very useful when it comes to the studying various optimization problems mainly solved via reinforcement learning and dynamic programming. MDPs are commonly used in different scientific areas like automated controls, robotics, manufacturing, and economics.

Generally speaking, an MDP is a very discrete time stochastic control process which at every step time, the process is in a certain state. Further, the decision maker chooses any action notably available at some certain state The process then responds by moving to the following state notably depending on the current stage as well as depending on the decision maker's stage. It should be noted that both elements are conditionally independent of any previous actions and states. In other words, that certain state of some MDP satisfies the overall Markov property.

It should be noted that Markov decision processes are, in fact, the big extension of Markov chains. However, these two differ from each other since there is the addition of different actions when it comes to the Markov decision processes. This means that in an MDP there are allowed different rewards as well as different choices notably giving motivation. It should be noted that if there is only a single action for every state, then all rewards will be the same. In this particular case, any Markov decision process will be reduced to a Markov chain.

Markov decision process is commonly a 5-tuple containing a finite set of different states and a finite set of different actions. Any Markov decision process also contains the probability function regarding the probability that some action in a specific state at a certain point in time will lead to another particular state at given time. An MDP also contains certain discount factor notably representing the overall differences existing in the importance between a present and future rewards. The last element of a Markov decision process is certain immediate rewards or some expected immediate reward notably received after certain transitioning from one state to another state due to a specific action.

When it comes to the core problems of MDPs, it is to find that certain policy for the specific decision maker. It is represented by the certain function specifying all actions that certain decision maker will choose when in a certain state. It should be noted that a Markov decision process is commonly combined with a certain policy in a manner that it fixes all actions for every state and the certain state. It leads to the resulting combination notably behaving as a Markov chain. The ultimate goal is to choose a certain policy which will most likely maximize the certain cumulative function of the specific random rewards. It is typically represented as the expected discounted sum over that potentially infinite horizon.

In the following section, you will see Python MDP toolbox with classes and functions in order to create Markov Decision Process. The classes are developed entirely based on the MATLAB MDP toolbox. The first array manipulation is done using NumPy. On the other hand, full sparse matrix support is done using SciPy's sparse package. There is also an optional linear programming support done using cvxopt. In the following section, you will see eight Markov decision implementation using Python. In order to do it this way, SciPy and NumPy must be installed on your system. If there are no these libraries installed on your system, use their documentation in order to get them.

First, you will install Python's toolbox PyPI. In order to get one, you just have to type pip install and pump toolbox. As soon as you have it, you will change it to the PyMDP Toolbox directory. You should install the repository via Setup tool, or you will not have needed administrative access. The following step is to clone the Git repository. After you done this you will follow step by step instructions. I assume you already know how to use Git, so that will not be a problem. The next step is to import the module and set up an example MDP problem by using a certain discount value of, let's say 0.9. You will solve it using the value iteration model and further check that optimal policy.

import mdptoolbox . example

P, R = mdptoolbox . example . forest ()

vi = mdptoolbox . mdp . ValueIteration ( P, R, 0.9 )

vi . run ()

vi . policy

Displaying the Relevant Documentation

import mdptoolbox

mdptoolbox? <ENTER>

mdptoolbox . mdp? <ENTER>

mdptoolbox . mdp . ValueIteration? <ENTER>

Python Markov decision process toolbox provides function as well as classes when it comes to the resolution of some discrete-time MDP. When it comes to the available modules, the toolbox includes Markov decision process algorithms, a function for working and validating an MDP and several examples of reward matrices and transitions notably forming a valid Markov decision process. When it comes to the using this certain documentation, it is available as both in pdf format and docstrings.

Use the Built-in Examples and Import Example Module

import mdptoolbox

import mdptoolbox . example

As soon as you imported the examples, it is not necessary to issue that import MDP toolbox command. It should be noted that certain code snippets will be indicated by certain three greater-than signs, so you do not get confused. In order to view doctrines of the certain value iteration of a specific class, you will run value interaction code.

x = 17

x = x + 1

x 18

When it comes to the available classes in Python MDP toolbox, you will find base MDP data, backward induction of finite horizon Markov decision process. You will also find classes including Q-learning Markov decision process, policy iteration MPD, value iteration MDP, modified policy iteration MDP and Gauss.Seidel value interaction Markov decision process. When it comes to the parameters available, you will find a discount factor, reward vectors and matrices, transitions or arrays, a different number of peri+dios, optional terminal rewards, ship check, attributes or data, optimal value function, optimal policy and used CPU time or time float.

import mdptoolbox, mdptoolbox . example

P, R = mdptoolbox . example . forest ()

fh = mdptoolbox . mdp . FiniteHorizon ( P, R, 0.9, 3 )

fh . run ()

fh . V array ([[ 2.6973, 0.81 , 0. , 0. ], [ 5.9373, 3.24 , 1. , 0. ], [ 9.9373, 7.24 , 4. , 0. ]])

fh . policy array ([[ 0, 0, 0 ], [ 0, 0, 1 ], [ 0, 0, 0 ]])

You are also able to set the Markov decision process to the silent mode using set silent command. You also can set the Markov decision process to the verbose mode using set verbose command.

run ()

setSilent ()

setVerbose ()

## Markov Decision Processes Parameters

In this section of the book, we will have a look at MDPs parameters including reward, discount, transitions, epsilon, skip check, maximum iteration and other. We have already know that the scope is to find that optimal policy notably a solution which specifies what we are supposed to do for each state other than that ultimate goal. Before we get into Python code for a Markov decision interface, you should get to know some of the most commonly used Markov decision parameters.

- Transitions: Arrays or transitions are different probability matrices. These can be easily defined in different ways. The simplest method is a numpy array, which has the shape of actions. However, there are also some other possibilities like tuple or list of different numpy objects of certain lengths. In this case, each element will contain that numpy array or matrix with the certain shape. This approach comes very usefully when certain transition matrices are, in fact, sparse. It should be noted that every action's transition should be index-able.

- Reward: Reward matrices are also called vectors. Just like the transition matrices, reward matrices also may be defined in different ways. The simplest method again is to form a numpy array with a certain shape. A list of lists may be used as well where every inner list may be composed of a certain outer list with a certain length of different actions. It should be noted that certain outer list may be replaced by some other object which can be indexed as a reward, object array of certain length of actions and numpy object.

- Discount: Discount factor represents certain per time-step discount factor on every future reward. It should be noted that valid values are commonly greater than zero and that they include value one. It the case when discount factor is one, the convergence cannot be assumed and there will be a certain warning displayed. It should be noted also that specific subclasses of Markov decision process may pass as none in the situation where the model does not use that certain discount factor.

- Epsilon: Epsilon when it comes to the Markov decision processes is certain stopping criterion. Using this parameter, that maximum change in a certain value function and each iteration is compared against certain epsilon function. The value function is considered to have certain coverage to the specific optimal function in the case when the certain change falls below the value. It should be noted that certain subclasses of

Markov decision process may easily pass to none in the situation where the model does not use that epsilon-optimal stopping criterion.

- Maximum Iteration: Maximum iteration parameter represents that maximum number of possible iterations. The Markov decision process model will be terminated as soon as this iteration comes at that stage where they simply elapse. This must be greater than zero in the case when specified. It should be noted that certain subclasses of Markov decision process may pass none in the situation when the model does not use that maximum number of possible iterations.
- Skip Check: We run this parameter in order to check on rewards and transitions arguments in order to make sure that they work properly and describe a certain valid Markov decision process. You may set this argument to true to skip this certain MDP check.

## A Markov decision process contains:

- A set of possible world states denoted as S
- A set of possible action detoned as A
- A real value reward function denoted as R

- A decsription T of every action's effects in every state

**Representing actions:**

- Deterministic Actions: For every state and action we need to specify a entirely new state.
- Stochastic Actions: For every state and action we need to specify a probability distribution over following states representing the certain distribution P(s' | s, a)

Some other common Markov decision parameters include policy zero which is a certain initial policy, attributes or data, eval type of the function used in order to evaluate that zero matrix in order to solve as a certain set of linear equations, tuple or the optimal value functions where every element is a certain effort corresponding to some expected value of being in certain state assuming that optimal policy is followed.

Other parameters used include time notably used to converge to some optimal policy, verbose, iteration showing CPU time, average time showing the average reward when it comes to the certain optimal policy, initial value showing the staring value function as vector of zeros and iter representing the total number of iterations notably taken in order to complete the computation. In the following section, you will get to know the code for a Markov decision process interface, the code used for the modified dict class and code for the Toy Markov decision process.

Markov Decision Process Interface

class MarkovDecisionProcess

def transition ( self, from _ state, action, to _ state )

raise NotImplementedError def initial _ state ( self )

raise NotImplementedError def reward ( self, state )

raise NotImplementedError def discount ( self, state )

raise NotImplementedError

Modified Dict Class

class SumDict ( dict )

```
def __setitem__ ( self, key, value )

self . has_key ( key )

value += self . get ( key ) dict . __setitem__ ( self, key, value )
```

## Toy Markov Decision Process

```
import numpy as np

class ToyMDP ( MarkovDecisionProcess )

def __init__ ( self )

self . world = np.array ([ [ -0.04, -0.04, -0.04, 1 ], [ -0.04, None, -0.04, -1 ], [-0.04, -0.04, -0.04, -0.04 ], ])

self . initial_state = ( 0, 0 )

self . finals = [( 0,3 ), ( 1,3 )]

self . actions = ( 'l', 'r', 'u', 'd' )

def __iter__ ( self )

def __init__( self, iterator, finals )

self . iterator = iterator

self . finals = finals def next ( self )

coords = self . iterator . coords
```

```
val = self.iterator.next()
return Iterator(self.world.flat, self.finals)
def _move(self, state, action)
    shape = self.world.shape
    next = list(state)
    elif action == 'l'
        self.world[state[0]][state[1]-1] != None)
            next[1] -= 1
    return tuple(next)
def successors(self, state, action
    d = SumDict()
    action == 'l
    d[self._move(state, 'l')] = 0.8
    d[self._move(state, 'u')] = 0.1
    d[self._move(state, 'd')] = 0.1
    return d
def transition(self, from_state, action, to_state)
    return self.successors(from_state, action)[to_state]
def initial_state(self)
```

```
return self . initial _ state

def reward ( self, state )

return self . world [ state [0]] [ state [1]]

def discount ( self )

return 1
```

When it comes to some probabilities where you have unknown rewards, Markov decision process is entirely a reinforcement learning problem. For this certain purpose, it is very useful if you use a method when you firstly defines a certain further function that corresponds to taking specific action and further continuing that optimally actions. It should be noted that in the certain case, the function would be unknown as well, but that experience during learning will be based on a set of actions and set of states put together with the certain outcomes which are state and actions being tried together at the same time. This is named Q-learning and in the following chapter, you will get to know this certain approach as well.

It should be noted that reinforcement learning could solve various Markov decision processes without any explicit specification when it comes to the different transitions probabilities. In this case, the values of different transition probabilities are only needed in policy and value iteration.

# Chapter 4 Approximate Dynamic Programming

In mathematics, computer science, economics, bioinformatics and many other scientific fields, dynamic programming is widely used in order to solve some complex problems mainly by breaking a problem down into a certain collection of some simpler problems. Dynamic programming further leads to solving there simpler problems by solving each of them once and then storing their overall solutions. Therefore, dynamic programming solves each problem instead of just re-computing their solutions. Using this approach, the models look up the some previously computed solution, notably leading to less computation time at the expense of some modest expenditure in storage space.

It should be noted that every sub-problem solution is mainly indexed in a certain manner mainly based on the certain values of its initial parameters. The technique of storing different solutions to some sub-problems instead of just re-computing them is named memorization. It should be noted that dynamic programming is also known as dynamic optimization. Algorithms obtained by this method are commonly used for optimization. A model is able to examine that previously solved sub-problems and it further combines their solutions in order to give the best solution for that given problem.

There are greedy algorithms as well that treat the solution as a sequence of certain steps and further picks that locally optimal choice at every step, which differs from dynamic algorithms. A greedy algorithm also does not guarantee that optimal solution, since picking some locally optimal choices commonly result in some bad global solution, but it is commonly faster to calculate. On the other hand, greedy models like Prim and Kruskal have proven to lead to that optimal solution.

Dynamic programming is also used when it comes to the counting the number of all solutions in addition to finding that optimal solution. For instance, counting the number of different ways a specific amount of changes may be made from an obtained collection of coins will be estimated using dynamic programming. Also counting the number of possible optimal solutions to the same coin problem will be estimated by dynamic programming.

Dynamic programming in addition to reinforcement learning is commonly used when it comes to the addressing different problems from a variety of fields including operations research, artificial intelligence, automatic control, and economy. Many problems in this specific field are commonly described by different continuous variables where reinforcement learning and dynamic programming can find that exact solution when it comes to some discrete cases. So, when it comes to the practical dynamic programming and reinforcement learning, an approximation is essential.

**Dynamic Programming:**

- Partitions a problem into overapping sub-problems
- Stores solutions of sub-problmes and avoids calculations of same quality twice
- Soecific mainly bottom up learning models in that manner that the smallest sub-problems are explicitly solved first and the results of these are used in order to construct solutions to progressively larger sub-instances

In the following section, you will see how to incorporate dynamic programming in order to get policy evaluation, value iteration, and policy iteration. Like I already mentioned Markov decision process problems can be solved using dynamic programming when we suppose that there is the state function denotes as P and certain rewards function denoted as R. When we wish to calculate the certain policy which maximizes that expected discounted reward we will use dynamic programming. The common family of models in order to calculate this policy require storage fo certain two arrays of some indexed value denoted as V. It should be noted that this value contains some real values and specific policy contains certain actions. At the end of this algorithm, you will see outcomes containing the solution V notably containing that discounted sum of different rewards specifically to be earned on average by simply following that solution obtained from a set of all states.

## Policy Evaluation

In this section of the book, you will see codes for policy evaluation using dynamic programming in Python. You will evaluate a certain policy when you gave already given environment as well as a full description of the overall environment's dynamics. In this case, the policy contains set of actions and set of states where shaped matrix will be representing this policy.

Running command evaluation, you will see the representation of all transition probabilities of certain environments. You will also stop the evaluation once your values function change come to a stage of being less than theta function. The discount factor is represented with a lambda function.

```
import numpy as np

import pprint

import sys

rom lib . envs . gridworld import GridworldEnv

pp = pprint . PrettyPrinter ( indent=2 )

env = GridworldEnv ()

def policy _ eval ( policy, env, discount _ factor = 1.0,
theta = 0.00001 )

V = np . zeros ( env.nS )

delta = 0

v = 0
```

You will perform a complete backup following the each state. You will start with that random or all zero value functions. The following step is to look at all possible following actions. Then you will calculate that expected values and o the every state you will look at the possible following states.

The following step is to calculate how much value function changed across every state. You will stop evaluating once your value function change to be below that threshold of theta when the delta is less than theta.

v += action _ prob * prob * ( reward + discount _ factor * V [ next_state ])

delta = max ( delta, np . abs ( v – V [ s ] ))

V [ s ] = v

return np . array ( V )

random _ policy = np . ones ([ env.nS, env.nA ]) / env . nA

v = policy _ eval ( random_policy, env )

print ( "Value Function:" )

print ( v )

print ("")

print ( "Reshaped Grid Value Function:" )

print (v . reshape ( env . shape ))

print ("")

Value Function:

[ 0. -13.99993529 -19.99990698 -21.99989761 -13.99993529 -17.9999206 -19.99991379 -19.99991477 -19.99990698 -19.99991379 -17.99992725 -13.99994569 -21.99989761 -19.99991477 -13.99994569 0. ]

Reshaped Grid Value Function: [[ 0. -13.99993529 -19.99990698 -21.99989761] [-13.99993529 -17.9999206 -19.99991379 -19.99991477] [-19.99990698 -19.99991379 -17.99992725 -13.99994569] [-21.99989761 -19.99991477 -13.99994569 0. ]]

The last step is testing. You should also make sure that the evaluated policy is matching that expected policy.

## Policy Iteration

In this section, you will see how to evaluate policy iteration using dynamic programming in Python. In this case, just as in the previous one, you will evaluate a policy when you have given a certain environment as well as that full description of the certain environment. In this case, a set of actions as well as a set of states will be representing the overall policy just like in policy evaluation. We will use command return representing a vector of a certain length and estimation command representing that value function. You will start with a random or all zero function like in the previous example.

import numpy as np

import pprint

import sys if

from lib . envs . gridworld import GridworldEnv

pp = pprint . PrettyPrinter ( indent=2 )

The following step is taken a form that policy evaluation example. You will also perform a full backup and look at the all possible following actions. Then you will see how much certain value function changed across every state. Further, you will calculate that expected value and stop evaluating as soon as your value function change is below a particular threshold where delta is less than theta.

V = np . zeros ( env.nS )

delta = 0

```
v = 0

v += action _ prob * prob * ( reward + discount _ factor *
V [ next_state ])

delta = max ( delta, np . abs (v – V [ s ]))

return np . array (V)

def policy _ improvement (env, policy _ eval _ fn = policy
_ eval, discount _ factor = 1.0 )
```

The following steps include policy improvement model. The codes iteratively evaluate as well as improve a certain policy until you find that optimal policy. Policy evaluation function is used and it takes three arguments including, evaluation, a certain discount factor, and policy. In this case, a certain discount factor is represented by lambda factor. You will also use return arguments as soon as you have a tuple policy containing V and policy. In this case, a policy is that optimal policy while a matrix of shape set of states and set of actions represents a certain situation where every set of states contains that valid probability distribution over different actions. In this case, V represent that value function for that optimal policy.

Further, you will start with a certain random policy and evaluate that current policy. Then you will be able to set false if you make changes to evaluate policy. The best action will be taken under that current policy. Further, you will find the best action using one-step Lookahead. You will notice that ties are resolved entirely arbitrarily. Then you will greedily update the current policy. In the case when the policy is entirely stable, you have found that optimal policy. On the other hand, you have to run return argument. The last step is to test the value function.

policy = np . ones ([ env.nS, env.nA ]) / env . nA

V = policy _ eval _ fn ( policy, env, discount _ factor )

policy policy _ stable

chosen _ a = np . argmax ( policy [ s ] )

action _ values = np . zeros ( env . nA )

action _ values[a] += prob * ( reward + discount _ factor * V [next _ state ]) best_a = np . argmax ( action _ values )

policy _ stable = False

policy [s] = np . eye ( env . nA)[ best _ a ]

policy _ stable

return policy

v = policy _ improvement ( env )

```
print ( "Policy Probability Distribution:" )

print (policy)

print ("")

print ( "Reshaped Grid Policy ( 0=up, 1=right, 2=down, 3=left ) :")

print (np . reshape (np . argmax (policy, axis=1), env . shape))

print ("")

print ( "Value Function:" )

print (v)

print ("")

print ( "Reshaped Grid Value Function:" )

print ( v.reshape(env.shape ))

print ("")
```

Policy Probability Distribution: [[ 1. 0. 0. 0.] [ 0. 0. 0. 1.] [ 0. 0. 0. 1.] [ 0. 0. 1. 0.] [ 1. 0. 0. 0.] [ 1. 0. 0. 0.] [ 1. 0. 0. 0.] [ 0. 0. 1. 0.] [ 1. 0. 0. 0.] [ 1. 0. 0. 0.] [ 0. 1. 0. 0.] [ 0. 0. 1. 0.] [ 1. 0. 0. 0.] [ 0. 1. 0. 0.] [ 0. 1. 0. 0.] [ 1. 0. 0. 0.]]

Reshaped Grid Policy ( 0=up, 1=right, 2=down, 3=left ): [[ 0 3 3 2 ] [0 0 0 2] [0 0 1 2] [0 1 1 0]]

Value Function: [ 0. -1. -2. -3. -1. -2. -3. -2. -2. -3. -2. -1. -3. -2. -1. 0.]

Reshaped Grid Value Function: [[ 0. -1. -2. -3.] [-1. -2. -3. -2.] [-2. -3. -2. -1.] [-3. -2. -1. 0.]]

Expected _ v = np . array ([ 0, -1, -2, -3, -1, -2, -3, -2, -2, -3, -2, -1, -3, -2, -1, 0 ]) np . testing . assert _ array _ almost _ equal ( v, expected _ v, decimal = 2 )

## Value Iteration

In order to get value iteration using dynamic programming, you will also have OpenAI environment. In this case, you will have the transition probabilities of an imported environment. You will use theta as stopping threshold. In the case when the value of every state changes to be less than theta, then you are done. The discount factor is represented in a lambda function. You will also use a helper function in order to calculate the value for every action in a certain state. State argument will be used in addition to the value notably used as an estimator with a vector of a certain length.

import numpy as np

```python
import pprint

import sys

sys.path.append("../")

from lib.envs.gridworld import GridworldEnv

pp = pprint.PrettyPrinter(indent=2)

env = GridworldEnv()

def value_iteration(env, theta = 0.0001, discount_factor = 1.0)

def one_step_lookahead(state, V)

A = np.zeros(env.nA)

A[a] += prob * (reward + discount_factor * V[next_state])

return A
```

The following step is to use stopping condition and update every state. You will also do a one-step lookahead in order to find the best possible actions. Further, you will calculate delta across every state notably seen so far and update that value function. The following is to perform checking if you can stop. Further, you will create a deterministic policy by using that optimal value function.

```
V = np.zeros(env.nS)

delta = 0

A = one_step_lookahead(s, V)

Best_action_value = np.max(A)

delta = max(delta, np.abs(best_action_value - V[s]))

V[s] = best_action_value

delta < theta

break

policy = np.zeros([env.nS, env.nA])

A = one_step_lookahead(s, V) best_action = np.argmax(A)

Policy[s, best_action] = 1.0

return policy, V

policy, v = value_iteration(env)

print("Policy Probability Distribution:")

print(policy)

print("")

print("Reshaped Grid Policy (0=up, 1=right, 2=down, 3=left):")
```

```python
print (np.reshape(np.argmax(policy, axis=1), env.shape))

print ("")

print ("Value Function:")

print (v)

print ("")

print ("Reshaped Grid Value Function:")

print (v.reshape( env.shape ))

print ("")
```

# Chapter 5 Integrating with OpenAI Gym

In this chapter, you will see how to integrate with OpenAI Gym. In the previous section, we have used OpenAI Gym in order to evaluate certain reinforcement learning parameters like value iteration and policy evaluation. OpenAI Gym has commonly used toolkit when it comes to the developing as well as comparing different reinforcement learning algorithms.

This toolkit makes no assumptions about the overall structure of a certain agent but it makes it compatible with various numerical computation libraries like Theano and TensorFlow. You will be able to use it directly from Python code as well as from other languages.

OpenAI Gym consists of two main parts, the service, and rich open-source library. The open-source library contains a set of numerous test problems as well as different environments which you can use in order to work out any of yours reinforcement learning models. These OpenAI Gym environments have that shared interface notably allowing you to write some general algorithms. On the other hand, OpenAI Gym service contains a site as well as an API notably allowing people to very meaningfully compare overall performance when it comes to their trained agents.

In order to get started, you need Python 3.5 or Python 2.7. You will fetch certain gym code. Later, you will run and install the toolkit. In order to do so, you will need recent pip version. You will be able to work on any package available.

git clone

cd gym

pip install -e . # minimal install

The following step is to run an environment from OpenAI Gym. You can use an environment for thousand time-steps. Further, you will render obtained environment following the every step.

import gym

env = gym . make ('CartPole-v0')

env . reset ()

env . render ()

env . step (env . action _ space . sample ())

Normally, you will end the simulation even before the cart-pole is allowed to entirely go off-screen. If you are interested in seeing some other environments form OpenAI Gym in action, then replace that cart-pole from the above with something else like MsPacman-v0 or MountainCr-v0. It should be noted that these two will require the Atari dependency. You also may use others as well like Hopper-v1 notably requiring the MuJoCo dependencies. It should be noted that all environments are descent from that base class.

It should be noted, if you are missing any dependencies, you are supposed to get that helpful error message notably telling you what you are missing. When it comes to the installing some missing dependencies the process is very simple. You will only need that MuJoCo license for certain Hopper-v1. The following step is to focus on observations.

If you ever want to perform better in order to take some random actions at every step, you will need to get to know what your actions are doing to certain environments. In order to do so, you have to run step function notably returning exactly what you need. You will get four values including reward, done, info and observation.

When you run step function, it will return value observation. It is entirely environment-specific object notably representing your observation when it comes to the certain environment like certain pixel data from a camera or joint velocities of a robot. On the other hand, you will also get reward function return representing an amount of reward specifically achieved by those previous actions. It should be noted that the scale would vary between different environments. However, the goal of increasing that total rewards always remains the same.

Another valuable function is done or Boolean used when it is the right time to reset that certain environment. Majority of tasks will be divided into some well-defined episodes like true and done. In this situation, true will indicate that the certain episode has terminated. Info function is that diagnostic information that comes very useful when it comes to the debugging. It can be used also for learning as well. On the other hand, official evaluations are not allowed to use this function in this specific learning problem.

The overall process will start when you call that reset function returning an initial observation. It should be noted that writing from that previous code would respect that done flag.

```
import gym

env = gym . make ('CartPole-v0')

observation = env . reset ()

env . render () print( observation )

action = env . action _ space.sample ()

observation, reward, done, info = env . step ( action )

print ( "Episode finished after {} timesteps" . format ( t+1 ))

break
```

As soon as you done and hit the break, you will have output where you are able to see where certain resets happened. It will look like this.


[-0.061586 -0.75893141 0.05793238 1.15547541]

[-0.07676463 -0.95475889 0.08104189 1.46574644]

[-0.0958598 -1.15077434 0.11035682 1.78260485]

[-0.11887529 -0.95705275 0.14600892 1.5261692]

[-0.13801635 -0.7639636 0.1765323 1.28239155]

[-0.15329562 -0.57147373 0.20218013 1.04977545]

Episode finished after exactly 14 time-steps

[-0.02786724 0.00361763 -0.03938967 -0.01611184]

[-0.02779488 -0.19091794 -0.03971191 0.26388759]

[-0.03161324 0.00474768 -0.03443415 -0.04105167]

In the previous example, you have been sampling that random actions form the certain environment's actions space. It should be noted that each environment comes with that first-class space very specific objects notably describing that valid observations and actions.

```
import gym
env = gym . make ('CartPole-v0')
print ( env . action _ space )
#> Discrete (2) print ( env . observation _ space )
#> Box (4,)
```

These discrete spaces will allow some fixed range when it comes to the non-negative numbers. In this certain case, a valid action will be either zero or one. You also have the box space notably representing that n-dimensional box. Therefore, valid observations, in fact, will come as an array containing four numbers. You are able to check that box bounds as well.

Print ( env . observation _ space . high)

#> array([ 2.4 , inf, 0.20943951, inf] )

Print ( env . observation _ space . low )

#> array ([-2.4 , -inf, -0.20943951, -inf])

This certain introspection comes as very useful in order to write some generic code for numerous different environments. The most common spaces are discrete and box functions. You are able to sample that space as well as to check that something belongs to that certain space.

from gym import spaces

space = spaces . Discrete (8) # Set with 8 elements {0, 1, 2, ..., 7}

x = space . sample ()

assert space . contains (x)

assert space . n = = 8

It should be noted that for CartPole-v0 will be one of the actions notably applying great force to the left. On the other hand, some of them will apply force to the right as well. It should be noted that the better your learning algorithm, the less you will have to try to interpret that numbers yourself. When it comes to the environment, the main purpose is to provide that large collection of different environments which expose that common interface that allow algorithmic comparison.

from gym import envs

print ( envs.registry . all ())

#> [ EnvSpec (DoubleDunk-v0 ), EnvSpec (InvertedDoublePendulum-v0), EnvSpec (BeamRider-v0), EnvSpec (Phoenix-ram-v0), EnvSpec (Asterix-v0), EnvSpec (TimePilot-v0), EnvSpec (Alien-v0), EnvSpec (Robotank-ram-v0), EnvSpec (CartPole-v0), EnvSpec (Berzerk-v0), EnvSpec (Berzerk-ram-v0), EnvSpec (Gopher-ram-v0)

This will give you that list of all spaces. Further, these will define that parameters needed for certain task, including that number of total trials required in order to run as well as to maximize the number of all steps. For instance, Hopper-v1 will define that environment where the main goal is to get that two-dimensional simulated robot. It should be noted that these environments are commonly treated as some opaque strings.

To ensure that valid comparison for some future environments, you will not change environments in a manner, which affects the overall performance. When it comes to the adding your own environment to the registry, you will run register command.

## Q-Learning Algorithms

In this section of the book, you will see how to explore a family of reinforcement learning algorithms called Q-learning models. It should be noted that these are a little bit different than other mainly policy-based models. Instead of starting with that complex as well as unwieldy deep neural network, you will begin by initially implementing that simple-lookup table version of the models.

The basic gist of every Q-learning model is to have a representation of different environmental states in addition to all possible actions in that states. You will learn the value of every action coming from the each state. This value q, in fact, is referred to that state-action value. In Q-learning, you will start by setting that state-action value to zero. You will go around as well as explore that certain state-action space.

The following step is to try certain action in a state, and you will evaluate that state. In the situation where a state leads to some undesirable outcome, you will reduce that Q value also known as a weight to the value of that action from a specific state.

Therefore, all other actions will have common greater value and they may be chosen the following time when you are examining that particular state. In the case when you are rewarded for taking a certain action, the overall weight of that action for that certain state will increase, so it is more likely that you will choose that state again.

It is important to remember when you update Q, you are also at the same time updating that previous state-action combination. It should be noted that you are able to update Q only after you have seen the results. In the following section, you will see how to implement Q-learning in Python.

```python
import numpy as np
```

```python
import matplotlib.pyplot as plt
from matplotlib.collections import LineCollection
```

The following step is to reward or connect certain graph. Then you will update state, the following state, action, gamma, and alpha. The following step is to renormalize that row to be between zero and one. You will also show all the greedy transversals and then cut off that final arrow.

```python
r = np.array([[-1, -1, -1, -1, 0, -1],
[-1, -1, -1, 0, -1, 100],
[-1, -1, -1, 0, -1, -1],
[-1, 0, 0, -1, 0, -1],
[0, -1, -1, 0, -1, 100],
[-1, 0, -1, -1, 0, 100]]).astype("float32")
q = np.zeros_like(r)
def update_q(state, next_state, action, alpha, gamma)
rsa = r[state, action]
qsa = q[state, action]
new_q = qsa + alpha * (rsa + gamma * max(q[next_state, :]) - qsa)
```

```python
q [state, action] = new_q

rn = q [state] [q[state] > 0] / np.sum ( q[state][q[state] > 0] )

q [state] [q[state] > 0] = rn

return r [state, action]

def show_traverse

range ( len ( q ))

current_state = i

traverse = "%i -> " % current_state

n_steps = 0

next_state = np.argmax (q[ current_state ])

current_state = next_state

traverse += "%i -> " % current_state

n_steps = n_steps + 1

traverse = traverse [:-4]

print ("Greedy traversal for starting state %i" % i)

print (traverse)

print ("")
```

The following step is to show all used or valid transitions. You will also invert that y axis for display. Then you will bump values for viz.

```
def show _ q ()

coords = np . array ([[2, 2],

[4, 2],

[5, 3],

[4, 4],

[2, 4],

[5, 2]])

Cords [:, 1] = max (cords [:, 1]) – cords [:, 1]

Plt. Figure (1, facecolor='w', figsize= (10, 8))

Plt . clf()

ax = plt . axes( [0., 0., 1., 1.] )

plt . axis ('off')

plt . scatter (cords [:, 0], cords [:, 1], c='r')

start _ idx, end_idx = np . where (q > 0)

segments = [[ coords[start], cords [stop]]

values = np . array (q[q > 0])
```

```
values = values

lc = LineCollection (segments, zorder=0,
cmap=plt.cm.hot_r)

lc . set _ array (values)

ax . add _ collection (lc)

verticalalignment = 'top'

horizontalalignment = 'left'

x = cords [i][0]

y = cords [i][1]

name = str (i)

y = y - .05

x = x + .05

elif i = = 3

y = y - .05

x = x + .05

elif i = = 4

y = y - .05

x = x + .05

y = y + .05
```

x = x + .05

plt . text (x, y, name, size=10

horizontalalignment = horizontalalignment

verticalalignment = verticalalignment

bbox = dict ( facecolor='w', edgecolor=plt.cm.spectral(float( len( cords )))

alpha=.6)) plt . show ()

The core algorithm will need that uncomment in order to see relevant plots within each monitoring. You will also show epsilon-greedy, show transverse and show Q. You should remember not to allow invalid moves at the very beginning and just take some random move. It should be noted that the goal state has reward hundred. The core algorithm will contain gamma, epsilon, alpha, a number of total states, actions and episodes.

gamma = 0.8

alpha = 1.

n _ episodes = 1E3

n _ states = 6

```
n_actions = 6

epsilon = 0.05

random_state = np.random.RandomState(1999)

states = list(range(n_states))

random_state.shuffle(states)

current_state = states[0]

goal = False

valid_moves = r[current_state]

random_state.rand()

actions = np.array(list(range(n_actions)))

actions = actions

[valid_moves == True]

actions = [actions]

action = actions[0]

next_state =

np.sum(q[current_state])

action = np.argmax(q[current_state])

actions = np.array(list(range(n_actions)))

actions = actions[valid_moves == True]
```

```
random_state.shuffle(actions)

action = actions[0]

next_state = action

reward = update_q(current_state, next_state, action,
alpha=alpha, gamma=gamma)

current_state = next_state

print(q)

show_traverse()

show_q()
```

# Chapter 6 Monte Carlo Methods

Monte Carlo methods are commonly used when it comes to the model which mimics certain policy iteration. Policy iteration commonly consists of two main steps including policy improvement and policy iteration.

Monte Carlo methods are used commonly in a stage of policy evaluation. In this certain stage, there is a given stationary or deterministic policy and the overall goal is to compute different function values out to find some good approximation to them in terms of all state-action pars.

In this case, we are assuming that the Markov Decision Process is finite and that there is that sufficient memory notably available in order to accommodate that action-values and that the certain problem is entirely episodic. It should be noted that after every episode the new starts from the random initial state. Further, the estimate of the specific value of already given state-action par can be easily computed by averaging that sample returns notably originating from a set of actions and set of states over a period of time.

When you have given sufficient time, this process may lead to constructing some precise estimate Q of the certain action-value function. Further, this finishes that description of that policy evaluation step.

When it comes to the policy improvement step in some standard policy iteration model, the following policy is commonly obtained by computing that greedy policy in respect to Q. When you have given a set of states, this policy will return an action which maximizes Q containing a set of states and set of actions.

In practice, we call this a lazy evaluation notably deferring the computation when it comes to the maximizing different actions to when they are required. It should be noted that this certain method works only in certain episodic problems and infinite and small Markov Decision Processes.

## Monte Carlo Prediction

In this section of the book, you will see how to integrate Monte Carlo prediction. The algorithm will be able to calculate the value function for some given policy using sampling. The policy will represent a function which maps an observation to a specific action probabilities. Here, we will also use OpenAI Gym in order to get needed environments. You will also number episodes needed to sample and lambda will represent a discount factor. It should be noted that value is a float while the state is a tuple.

```
import gym
import matplotlib
import numpy as np
import sys
from collections import defaultdict
from lib.envs.blackjack import BlackjackEnv
from lib import plotting

matplotlib.style.use('ggplot')

env = BlackjackEnv()

def mc_prediction(policy, env, num_episodes, discount_factor=1.0)

returns_sum = defaultdict(float)

returns_count = defaultdict(float)

V = defaultdict(float)

Print("\rEpisode {}/{}.".format(i_episode, num_episodes), end="")

Sys.stdout.flush()
```

The following step is to keep track of count and sum of returns for every state in order to calculate an average. You will use an array in order to save all returns. The next step is to get the final value function. Then, you will print every episode which comes very useful for debugging. Further, you will generate an episode. It should be noted that an episode, in fact, is an assay including reward, state, and action.

episode = [ ]

state = env . reset

action = policy (state)

next _ state, reward, done, _ = env . step (action)

episode . append ((state, action, reward))

state = next _ state

first _ occurence _ idx

G = sum ([x[2]*(discount _ factor**i)

Returns _ sum [state] += G

Returns _ count [state] += 1.0

V [state] = returns _ sum [state]

Returns _ count [state]

return V

def sample _ policy (observation)

V _ 10k = mc _ prediction ( sample_policy, env, num_episodes=10000 )

Plotting . plot _ value _ function (V _ 10k, title="10,000 Steps" )

V _ 500k = mc _ prediction (sample _ policy, env, num _ episodes=500000)

Plotting . plot _ value _ function (V_500k, title="500,000 Steps")

The next step is to find all states notably visited in this certain episode. You will also convert every state to a tuple so you can use it as a dict key. Further, you will find that first occurrence as a certain state in that episode and sum all reward since that first occurrence. The next step is to calculate that average return for this certain state over all sampled states.

## Monte Carlo Tree Search

When it comes to the subject of game artificial intelligence, it all begins with that perfect information. These, in fact, are turn-based games where players have no that information hidden from other players, so there is no that element of chance when it comes to the game mechanics.

In this types of games everything is fully determined, so Monte Carlo tree can be easily constructed containing all possible outcomes as well as a value notably assigned corresponding to a loss or a win for players. Finding that possible play is a matter of doing a certain search on a tree. It is a certain method of choice and picking that maximum and minimum value. The algorithm is called Minimax.

In order to incorporate simple Monte Carlo tree search in Python, you will need Board class that has a purpose of encapsulating the rules of the certain game. Board class only cares about the artificial intelligence model rather than being concerned with Monte Carlo class. It obtains information about the certain game.

class Board (object)

def start (self)

```
pass

def current_player(self, state)

pass

def next_state(self, state, play)

pass

def legal_plays(self, state_history)

pass def winner(self, state_history)

pass
```

It should be noted that you will require certain state data structure containing equivalent states which have that same value. You can use flat tuples as your state data structure. Certain AI class will be constructed using certain interface.

```
class MonteCarlo(object)

def __init__(self, board, **kwargs)

pass

def update(self, state)

pass

def get_play(self)
```

```
pass

def run _ simulation (self)

pass

class MonteCarlo (object)

def __init__ (self, board, **kwargs)

self . board = board

self . states = [ ] def update (self, state)

self . states . append (state)
```

The next step is to move towards bookkeeping and initialization. The board object is the place where AI will start obtaining some information about the game. Therefore, you will need to store that information as well as to keep track of certain state data as you get it.

# Chapter 7 Temporal Difference Learning

Temporal Difference methods or learning is certain prediction based machine learning approach. It is mainly used for reinforcement learning.The approach, in fact, is a certain combination of Monte Carlo methods and dynamic programming. Temporal difference greatly resembles Monte Carlo methods since it also allows learning by sampling certain environments according to the specific policy. O the other hand, the temporal difference is related to dynamic programming since is also approximates some of its current estimate notably based on some previously learned estimates specifically known as the process of bootstrapping.

The temporal different model is commonly related to temporal difference model when it comes to the animal learning. This is a certain prediction method since temporal difference learning considers that numerous subsequent predictions to be related in some manner. When it comes to the supervised predictive learning, an agent is able to learn form observed values and prediction is made when a certain observation is available. On the other hand, overall prediction mechanism is further adjusted in order to better match a certain observation. Temporal difference learning is all about adjusting predictions to match other more accurate prediction regarding the future. In the following section, you will see how to integrate Q-learning solution using temporal difference method in Python. In order to start, you will cerate an epsilon-greedy policy notably based on some given q-function and epsilon. You will use a Q dictionary that maps from a certain state to certain action-values. It should be noted that every value represents a certain numpy array of a certain length. Epsilon is a function representing that probability to select some random actions. The following step is to get a total number of actions in the certain environment.

% matplotlib inline

import gym

import itertools

import matplotlib

import numpy as np

import pandas as pd import sys

sys . path . append ("../")

from collections import defaultdict

from lib . envs . cliff _ walking import CliffWalkingEnv

```
from lib import plotting

matplotlib.style.use('ggplot')

env = CliffWalkingEnv()

def make_epsilon_greedy_policy(Q, epsilon, nA)

def policy_fn(observation)

A = np.ones(nA, dtype=float) * epsilon / nA

Best_action = np.argmax(Q[observation])

A[best_action] += (1.0 - epsilon)

return A

return policy_fn
```

The Q-learning model is entirely off-policy temporal difference able of finding that optimal greedy policy while following that epsilon-greedy policy. The following step is to find the total number of episode notably needed to run for and to find that lambda time discount factor. Alpha will determine a certain learning rate while epsilon represents that chance when it comes to the sampling some random actions. It should be noted that a float will be between zero and one.

```
def q _ learning ( env, num _ episodes, discount _
factor=1.0, alpha=0.5, epsilon=0.1 )

Q = defaultdict ( lambda: np . zeros (env . action _ space.n
))

stats = plotting . EpisodeStats

( episode _ lengths=np.zeros (num _ episodes)

Episode _ rewards=np . zeros (num _ episodes))

policy = make _ epsilon _ greedy _ policy ( Q, epsilon,
env.action _ space.n )

sys . stdout . flush ()

state = env . reset ()

action _ probs = policy (state)

action = np . random . choice (np.arange
(len(action_probs)), p=action_probs)

next _ state, reward, done, _ = env . step (action)

stats . episode _ rewards [i_episode] += reward

stats . episode _lengths [i_episode] = t

best _ next _ action = np . argmax (Q[next_state])

td _ target = reward + discount _ factor * Q [next_state]
[best_next_action]

td _ delta = td _ target – Q [state][action]
```

Q [state] [action] += alpha * td _ delta

break

state = next _ state

return Q, stats

Q, stats = q _ learning (env, 500)

Episode 500/500

Plotting . plot _ episode _ stats (stats)

In this certain temporal learning example, you will get that action-value function. You will also obtain that nested dictionary notably mapping states including action and action-value. It should be noted that you have to keep track of all useful statistics like episode lengths and episode rewards. The next step is to print out that episode notably very useful for debugging and to update TD.

# Conclusion

Reinforcement learning is a wide area of machine learning mainly inspired by another scientific field, behaviorist psychology. Reinforcement learning is commonly concerned with how certain software agents can take different actions in different environments in order to maximise that notion when it comes to the cumulative reward. Reinforcement learning is also one of the most active areas when it comes to the artificial intelligence since its computational approach is to focus on whereby a reinforcement agent acts toward maximizing that total amount of rewards notably received when interactions with the complex as well as the uncertain environment.

The overall concept of reinforcement learning has reached its peak only a couple of years ago even though artificial intelligence research has bee present in the pasty sixty years as the wide field of machine learning. Since this reinforcement learning peak, it is more than apparent that the technology industry has been greatly updating robots as well as presenting to us some very innovative machines. We really did not know that it is possible to design these machines notably able of learning by themselves with no human intervention.

This is what excites us the most, and solving some complex learning problems through reinforcement learning is simply the future. It is more than apparent that artificial intelligence techniques will shape the world that we know and reinforcement learning is a great part of different machine learning techniques as well as a great part of the artificial intelligence approach.

Reinforcement learning encompasses both adaptive behaviors in terms of rational beings and science in specific environments as well as certain computational methodology in order to find that best behavior when it comes to some challenging problems, adaptive behavior of different intelligent agents and optimization. This book welcomes you to the world of reinforcement learning by presenting you the technology lying behind self-driving cars, programs particularly able to beast world champions and being robots specifically the future and not a part of futuristic movies, not anymore.

Printed in Great Britain
by Amazon